How *to* Keep Your
Teenager
from Driving
You Crazy

How *to* Keep Your
Teenager
from Driving
You Crazy

*A Proven Program for Enforcing Limits
and Restoring Peace to Your Family*

Paula Stone Bender, Ph.D.

CB
CONTEMPORARY BOOKS

Library of Congress Cataloging-in-Publication Data

Bender, Paula Stone, 1943–
    How to keep your teenager from driving you crazy: a proven
program for enforcing limits and restoring peace to your family /
Paula Stone Bender.
       p.   cm.
    Includes index.
    ISBN 0-8092-2390-2
    1. Parents and teenager. 2. Adolescent psychology. I. Title.

HQ799.15.B46   2000
649′.125—dc21

                                    00-22656

Cover design by Peter Chu
Cover illustration copyright © Elwood H. Smith
Interior design by kalzub design

Published by Contemporary Books
A division of NTC/Contemporary Publishing Group, Inc.
4255 West Touhy Avenue, Lincolnwood (Chicago), Illinois 60712-1975 U.S.A.
Printed in the United States of America
International Standard Book Number: 0-8092-2390-2
01 02 03 04 05 06 MV 15 14 13 12 11 10 9 8 7 6 5 4 3 2

CONTENTS

Acknowledgments

My teenage son, Sean, deserves major credit for all his help with this book. Throughout the writing process, he served as a consultant, contributor, and reviewer. His insights and suggestions helped give this book a teenage voice and perspective. A special thanks to him for so generously contributing his time and effort.

Many others were there for me as well. My husband, Bob, and my older son, Mike, offered support. Mike provided examples of using a contract in our home laboratory as well. My sister, Ann Stone, shared her experiences working with teens and helped me organize my thoughts. Colleagues and friends such as Paula Eastman and Susan Phillips gave me reassurance and pushed me just enough to keep me going. My mom and dad also deserve credit. Although they didn't use the term *contract* with me as a teenager, as I look back I realize they used with all their children a positively based set of principles that had a similar effect to a contract.

My agent, Joel Fishman, helped me to focus my ideas and, as always, championed my efforts and approach. My editor, Judith McCarthy, provided guidance and welcome suggestions concerning each phase of the book's development. I greatly appreciate their efforts.

A final thanks to all the teenagers and their families who over the years have shown me that a contract that specifies rules, rewards, and punishments can work to help everyone get along better and reach a peaceful accord.

INTRODUCTION: SAVING YOUR SANITY

Is your teen driving you up the wall? Does your teen spend hours talking on the phone to friends while virtually ignoring your existence? Does your daughter obsess over every detail? Does she worry about what her classmates think of her but disregard your input altogether? Does your son beg for an extended curfew only to come home late proving he can't handle his new freedom? Does your daughter insist she's responsible and will call to let you know where she is but forget to do so? Does your son guarantee that he's got school under control all on his own and then bring home awful interim grades? Does your teen promise to come home to baby-sit or feed the dog but fail to do so? Does your daughter drag her feet every morning barely making it to school on time? Do your teens assure you they're studying when instead they're on the computer for hours sending E-mail or playing games? Does your son beg out of the chores you've asked him to do because he's too tired, only to leave to play basketball with a buddy who's just dropped over?

Believe it or not, your teens aren't being irresponsible on purpose. In fact, even though your teenager may not show it, she needs and wants your support, encouragement, and help learning how to become more responsible for herself. But how do you help her when her behavior is so maddening, robbing you of the last shreds of your sanity?

Although it may be tempting to grit your teeth and try to ride it out, I strongly oppose using a passive approach in raising teenagers. I've found it's nonproductive and nonrealistic. For one thing, adolescence lasts too long to sit by and do nothing. Officially there are seven teenage years—13, 14, 15, 16, 17, 18, and 19—adding up to 364 weeks or 2,557 days (allowing for two leap years). That's a lot of years, weeks, and days to be driven crazy. Ask any parents of a teenager and they'll tell you it feels even longer than that. In fact, most parents feel the time lasts considerably longer than the time it took to build Stonehenge, the Great Pyramids of Egypt, and the Great Wall of China combined. But no matter how long it lasts, parents still have to find some way to stay sane and coexist with their teens.

Any way you look at it, that's really the only choice *you* have. You, yes *you,* had these kids, and now they're teens and, let's face it, you're stuck. So you might as well try to make the best of this seven-year stretch. But how? Believe it or not, there are some things you can do to stay sane at least some of the time, and teach your teens to become more responsible while you're at it.

As a clinical psychologist for the past 25 years, I have helped hundreds of families cope with exasperating teen behavior, reach détente, and keep the peace. And as a mother of two teenage boys myself, I have grappled on a daily basis with the challenges of raising teens. Experience at the office and on the home front, as well as documented scientific research, has convinced me that the most effective way to raise kids is for parents to initiate action and negotiate a positively based behavior contract with their teens. This kind of contract provides incentives for following the rules and taking responsibility for one's own behavior as well as punishments for breaking the rules. Over time, using this kind of contract can help teens become more accountable for their behavior. A mutually agreed-upon contract can bring more peace to almost any home. Over the years I've been pleasantly surprised by the number of different kinds of problems a negotiated behavior contract helped solve. Although some teens need more help than a contract can deliver, negotiating a contract rarely makes matters *worse*. Contracts can alleviate some problems that troubled teens experience and can be used in conjunction with other forms of medical and psychological assistance when necessary.

In this book I share my formula for devising a successful behavior contract that you can use every day with your teens. This formula is based on extensive, longstanding scientific research into effective parenting styles as well as what techniques can be used to motivate teens to learn and change. (See Appendix D for resources.) In a nutshell, a successful contract spells out what teens must do to earn positive incentives and/or privileges such as money, free time, and outings with friends. Using this kind of contract encourages teens to follow school, safety, and family rules. For example, it can motivate your teen to get up and out in the morning, to act civilly to other family members, to go to school and finish schoolwork, to come home on time, and to call when he or she is running late. Your contract will also specify the negative consequences for breaking the rules, whether it's losing privileges or being grounded.

To bring my ideas to life, I'll include case studies of my own, very real clients (names changed, of course), and my own experience as a parent of teens. Thoughts and insights of friends and colleagues will be included as well. I'll look at how to keep and use a sense of humor when raising teenagers or, perhaps more accurately, when teenagers are raising *you*. Parenting without a sense of humor has never been an option for me.

Most important, I'll provide you with a step-by-step approach to take with your teens as you create a living, breathing behavior contract. I'll share practical guidelines to help you get along better with your teenager.

I'm well aware of how challenging, confusing, and time-consuming raising a teenager can be. So please allow me to pat you on the back and tell you how wonderful it is that you care about your teenagers, want to help them gain their independence, and are willing to take the time and effort to learn about and initiate a contract with them. If they haven't already, someday they'll realize how lucky they are to have caring, concerned parents.

This book is intended as a guide for parents with children ages 12 to 17. Using a contract can help your teen meet many of the challenges and hurdles he faces at home, in school, and in society. A contract can come to your teen's aid as he struggles to adjust to middle school, drive safely, deal with peer pressure, handle temptation, face increased academic difficulty, reconnect with the family, or look ahead to higher education. As you read this book you'll get ideas about how to use a contract to empower your teen as she assumes ever-increasing responsibility for her own behavior.

A contract will work in small as well as large families with either one parent or two. If you're a one-parent family, finding a supportive buddy who is available to share your adventures is most helpful. In a two-parent family a united front is the ideal situation; however, if one parent balks at a contract, the other parent can get the ball rolling as long as the nonparticipating parent doesn't sabotage it. In time the nonenthusiastic parent comes around and embraces the contract, usually because it becomes obvious that the contract is working.

Since all suggestions throughout the book apply to both teenage girls and boys, I alternate using female and male pronouns. All references to "he" or "she" apply to both genders.

This book is divided into five parts. Part I, Chapters 1 and 2, explains how to lay the groundwork for your contract by gaining perspective and focusing on the positive. In Part II, Chapters 3 through 5, you learn how to choose the components of your contract—rules, rewards, and discipline. Part III covers drafting a viable contract that's just right for your family. Chapter 6 helps you decide on the best contract format for your teen. Making your contract part of your family's life is the subject of Chapter 7. Chapter 8 gives you tips to follow as you negotiate your contract with your teen. Part IV looks at your contract in action. Chapter 9 focuses on using your contract to increase good behavior; while Chapter 10 covers handling contract problems and violations. Chapter 11 explores how to teach your teen personal responsibility. And finally, in Part V, Chapters 12 through 14 will help you take stock of changes, decide if your teenager needs extra help, and look ahead to your future with the contract.

Although each family's contract is unique, there are some general rules your family will benefit from following. Guidelines for developing your contract are presented as you work through this book. In fact, I'll show you each step you need to take to put a negotiated behavior contract into action. I'll encourage you to go at your own pace and take your time. To maximize your success, I recommend that you read through the book sequentially, chapter by chapter. You're not expected to change overnight or to become a perfect parent. But do sincerely try to put the techniques into action. If you discuss contracts with your teen, but never draft and negotiate one, you're wasting your time. The bottom line is that you must take concrete action if any change is to occur. The pages that follow outline and discuss everything you need to know and do to create a workable, successful contract. So please be patient, hang in there, and follow along with each step of the book.

Spend as much time on each part as you need. On the average, families find that working through Parts I through III and getting their contract ready for action takes three to four weeks. After that they're ready to start with Part IV and use the contract with their teen. Most families find it helpful to cover the chapters in Part IV during the first month of their contract. After three or four months, many parents feel ready to move on to Part V and evaluate the contract and decide where to go next.

Although contracting may sound like a lot of work, most of my clients are willing to put in the effort because the payoff is so great. Your contract will provide an environment that encourages your teen to develop the independence and responsibility she'll need for the future. You'll be pleasantly surprised at how much a negotiated behavior contract will improve your relationship with your teen. For example, your teen will enjoy the feeling of succeeding in school, finishing projects, and turning assignments in on time. She will be pleased with herself that she can act responsibly and get home on time. She'll relish the ability to save up for something rather than squander all her money the moment she receives it. So what are you waiting for? It's a perfect time to get started and rediscover the great person your teenager is.

How *to* Keep Your Teenager *from* Driving You Crazy

PART I

LAYING THE GROUNDWORK FOR A MORE PEACEFUL HOME

I

Gaining Perspective

Are your teens robbing you of your sanity? Do you feel perplexed and confused about how to be an effective parent? Do you find yourself clueless about how to help your teens through their wonder years, not to mention how to survive these turbulent times yourself? If you feel bewildered, take comfort. Help is on the way.

My experiences as a psychologist and mother have convinced me that to be effective, parents must initiate action and negotiate a positively based behavior contract with their teens. In this book I'll show you how to develop such a contract and put it into action.

WHAT IS A BEHAVIOR CONTRACT?

A behavior contract is a written agreement between you and your teen that specifies what rules your teen is expected to follow and what kinds of incentives and rewards he can earn for following them. In addition to this positive aspect, the contract also specifies the negative consequences—punishments—your teen will receive if he does not follow the rules. For example, your daughter may be able to earn extra money or free time for finishing her schoolwork. She may earn the privilege of extra phone time for getting along with her younger brother. On the other hand, if your son breaks an important rule and comes home 30 minutes late, he may receive the punishment of an earlier curfew for several nights. If your daughter spends time on the phone instead of doing her homework, she may lose phone privileges for a day or two.

Contracts can come to the rescue in a number of situations such as jump-starting a behavior that isn't happening, breaking a bad habit, encouraging an ongoing good behavior, or teaching a new one. Contracts can create an environment in which your rules are explicit. When expectations are clearly understood, conflicts over the daily business of living are reduced and thus the doors open for the possibility of communication and problem solving between parent and teen.

As a final benefit, the contract you'll be learning about using will provide an environment that helps your teen gradually become more responsible and independent as he moves toward adulthood.

Although a positive-based behavior contract can be effective in a variety of situations, if your teen displays chronic or serious antisocial behaviors, is sexually promiscuous, and/or has a substance abuse problem, you'll need more than a contract to turn things around. In fact, I'd recommend outside professional help now before things get worse. You may want to turn to Chapter 13, which contains information on when and how to get extra help.

Using the guidelines I'll give you, you'll develop a contract that fits your family's unique needs. Although you are in charge of the contract process and have the final say, you'll get your teen's input as you negotiate the terms of the contract before putting it into action. You should see positive results in two or three weeks. And, over time, the contract will teach your teen to behave responsibly and to become accountable for his behavior.

As a first step you need to lay the groundwork for developing your contract. This chapter helps you to adopt a realistic perspective on what your teen is going through and what parenting style works best.

Adopt a Realistic Perspective

Kids grow up so quickly. Before you know it and certainly before you're ready for it, your sweet, loving, pleasant, reasonably well-disciplined child turns 13. Take a deep breath. The teenage years have begun.

Brace yourself. Expect the unexpected. In your eyes your teen's behavior is likely to seem inconsistent, unpredictable, and irrational. Grappling with the mysteries of your teenager's behavior is *normal*.

When you consider all the changes and confusion your teens are going through, it's no wonder some of their behavior is maddening. Your teen goes from being a child to being a young adult capable of producing children. This cataclysmic change takes place outside the control of the teen or his parents. Hormones follow their preprogrammed trajectory, and all anyone can do is hold on for dear life and watch and wait.

Socially whatever is going on is just as great a mystery, with the implicit rules of "cool" changing daily, if not hourly. What other group would so readily admit and embrace paradoxical thinking with such statements as "She's so mean but so popular" or "I think I'm too nice to have a girlfriend; the girls all seem to want boyfriends who treat them like dirt."

School accomplishments, once a badge worn proudly, are often ridiculed, causing some students to keep them as hidden as possible. In some cases, teens purposely become bad students just to fit in. Plus, academics get tougher and other activities are easier to excel in and/or enjoy. Listening to music, watching television, or talking on the phone takes a lot less mental energy than studying for a history exam or a math test.

Against this chaotic backdrop, teens are faced with even greater, more available temptation than ever before. According to the May 9, 1999, issue of *Newsweek* magazine, in 63 percent of American homes both parents work, leaving their teens alone after school and into the evening. Teens can obtain drugs and alcohol at an early age. In addition to violent video games, the computer provides access instantly to antisocial information of all kinds. So especially for teens who are by themselves a great deal, it can be hard to stay away from all the negative influences so readily available.

What's more, teens are expected to develop compassion and empathy, to adopt a value system that champions the rights of self and others, and to handle disappointment and frustration with self-control and maturity.

To sum it up, in spite of all this turmoil, a teenager's *job* is to become increasingly competent and responsible, a feat that can be achieved only by mastering a series of small steps over a long period of time.

As if all these changes weren't enough, as teens develop mentally they become increasingly capable of questioning their parents' decisions. They begin challenging, fighting back—sometimes justifiably and sometimes for its own sake, but almost always when they feel their parents are being arbitrary or just plain wrong. Although this newfound skill on their part makes it more difficult to negotiate with them, it's important not to take it personally. Instead, rejoice. Your teens are flexing their newly acquired intellectual muscles. They're getting more savvy. They're on the right path toward becoming independent, functional adults. In many ways history is repeating itself. Just remember back to when you were a teen and how well you communicated with your parents.

Looking Back to Your Own Teen Years

Were you a perfect teen? Of course you weren't. *No one* was. When I remember back to my adolescence, I have to admit that I engaged in my share of typical nerve-racking teenage antics. Even though I needed my parents' support and attention, I was careful not to let them know it.

What do you remember about being a teenager? Do you look back to your adolescence fondly? Maybe that's because it was terrific and fun or maybe that's because time helps erase painful memories and leaves the more pleasant memories intact.

But why dwell on the negative experiences of the past? Who needs to be plagued by everything that went wrong? But keep in mind that selective memory can shut out the problems altogether, and this can do parents of teens a disservice. If parents don't remember how up and down and fraught with confusion these years were for them, they're apt to have difficulty relating to their teen's problems.

As painful as it may be, try to think back to the downs of your own teen years as well as the ups. Reminding yourself of the best and worst may help you develop a more compassionate perspective on what your teenager is going through.

Here are some guidelines to follow to help you reconnect with your inner teenager. Spend time reminiscing about being a teen. Talk about what it was like to be a teenager with your spouse, a sibling, or a close friend. Look at a scrapbook or a yearbook. Call a high school friend. Reminisce about your worries, your concerns, and your ups and downs. Talk to your own parents if possible about how they felt about parenting you as a teenager—their frustrations and challenges as well as the good times. Do whatever it takes to help you to go back in time.

Your own memories will help, but remember that no matter how empathic you are to the plight of your teenager's current phase of life or how in touch you are with your own past, it's still tough to be a good parent to a teen. After all, it's a different world now.

COMMON PARENTING PITFALLS

Faced with the baffling complexities of adolescence, it's easy for parents to fall into traps. Some parents get desperate and resort to an overly restrictive, dictatorial stance, while others adopt a laissez-faire approach and let their teen do whatever he wants. Still others end up vacillating between these two approaches. Unfortunately, each of these styles is doomed to failure. Let's look at three different families.

The Stantons

When Sue Stanton described her relationship with her 13-year-old son, Tom, it became clear that she was using a dictatorial, overly vigilant approach in hopes of keeping him out of trouble. Responding to the alarmist articles she had read about teenagers spinning out of control, Sue regularly searched Tom's room looking for evidence of drug or alcohol use. She insisted on searching through his backpack for clues that would prove he was ditching school or failing a class. As Tom saw it, "She's always in my face, always asking questions." Understandably Tom resented this intrusion into his space and privacy. It upset him and made him angry that his mother didn't seem to trust him; as far as he knew he had never given her reason to doubt him. He told me that sometimes it felt like instead of a mom he lived with a prison warden.

The O'Connells

Elaine and Jim O'Connell went in the opposite direction. As their daughters, Becky, 14, and Sarah, 16, became more independent and strong-willed, the O'Connells assumed a laissez-faire parenting stance. Jim felt that the girls resented his interference, so he bowed out. In his defense, Elaine added, "I guess we've done all we can. The girls don't seem to need us anymore. I guess they're ready to be on their own." Like many other teens in this situation, Becky and Sarah perceived their parents as aloof and not caring. They felt rejected. As I talked to Becky and Sarah it became clear that no matter how they acted, they weren't ready to be on their own and in fact very much wanted their parents' guidance and support.

The Espinozas

Waffling between stretches of laissez-faire punctuated with attempts at tight control is also a miserable combination that strips parents of their legitimate authority, as Maria and Keith Espinoza found out. In their eyes their son Wayne, 15, got to do pretty much what he wanted. And while he did comply with the few rules they set (weekend curfews and calling in when running late), they felt his attitude needed some work. On a recent Friday night, Wayne and Keith got into an argument at dinner over whether Wayne was studying enough to get into college. Wayne reminded his dad he had a B+ average. To which Keith replied, "Well, you can't get complacent. School is going to get harder and you'll have to take the SATs and AP courses." At this point, Wayne was in a hurry to leave and meet his friends. Keith wanted to keep talking. When Wayne explained he had to go, Keith shot back that his friends had become more important than his family or his schoolwork and that Wayne was grounded until he sorted this out, developed a better attitude, and showed some respect for his parents. Wayne was furious. As he saw it, he'd kept curfew and his parents had no reason to revoke his privilege of going out with friends. To Wayne, his parents' actions were inconsistent, maddening, and confusing. Many teens in this situation learn to ride out their parents' vacillations. They view their parents as arbitrary and irrational. Over time many teens in this situation grow away from their parents as their resentment and rebellion grow.

Although Sue Stanton, the O'Connells, and the Espinozas cared about their teens, their parenting approaches sent their children a different message. As a result, their teens felt mistrusted, rejected, and unloved. Like many other teens, they missed the understanding and support they so badly needed and wanted from their parents. In fact, surveys reported in a May 1999 issue of *Newsweek* found that the number-one concern of teens is that their parents are not there to provide guidance and support.

AUTHORITATIVE PARENTING

In spite of how he may act toward you or how crazy he may drive you, your teen wants you around—just not in your old role as supervisor and decision maker but rather in a new role as consultant and guide. In addition, your teen wants a home environment that's predictable and supportive—a safe haven with explicit reasonable rules. Study after study demonstrate that an authoritative approach to parenting is most successful in raising teens. According to experts on adolescence such as Lawrence Steinberg and David Elkind, the basic tenets of authoritative parenting include loving and trusting your adolescent, setting clear reasonable limits, balancing control with independence, being firm and fair, and accepting her as an individual. While many parents try to follow these guidelines, their attempts often prove futile and they lose their resolve. This was the case when Claire and Jack Daley came to see me. Like many parents, Jack and Claire had tried a number of different approaches with their teens Scott, 14, and Terry, 17. They'd had mixed success. Most recently they had tried to put the tenets of authoritative parenting into practice. Completely frazzled and at their wit's end after a harrowing Sunday evening, they called me, certain that they were the worst parents in the world and/or that they had the worst kids in the world or maybe both.

I asked the Daleys to fill me in on what they called their most recent parenting disaster. Concerned that they weren't being understanding and supportive enough of their children, Claire and Jack decided that instead of harping about homework all weekend long, they'd give Terry and Scott more freedom. They'd let them go out provided the kids came home on time and promised to have their homework completed by Sunday evening. Terry and Scott were very enthusiastic about this plan, promising they'd get their schoolwork done all on their own. In Scott's words, it was "no problemo." Terry confided that it really felt good to be trusted. Claire and Jack were elated. Maybe this was the end of bickering, nagging, and begging. Maybe Terry and Scott were ready to take responsibility for themselves.

Both teens most likely were sincere in their intentions to follow through, but as the weekend unfolded and opportunities to do things they wanted came along, they both put homework out of their minds. Before they knew it, it was dinnertime on Sunday. Terry had promised to visit her friend Jenny for a while that evening to talk about "serious boyfriend stuff" and figured she could do her homework afterward. Scott hadn't considered homework when he made plans to play a computer game on-line with his friend Roger. Since their parents had been so understanding on Friday and so nice during the weekend, Terry and Scott were certain their parents would understand why they hadn't gotten around to their schoolwork. After all, both were good students. It wasn't as if they were flunking out.

Sunday night dinner began pleasantly enough with each family member recounting the fun they'd had during the weekend. Terry offered that it was one of the best weekends ever and Scott concurred. Claire and Jack shared how relieved they were that they didn't have to worry about schoolwork getting done and how nice it was not to nag and bicker all weekend. Terry agreed and said that just as she had promised, she'd be starting her homework after she got back from Jenny's house.

Confused, Jack asked, "Excuse me, Terry, did I just hear you say that you haven't even started your homework yet?" "Don't worry, Dad, I'll have plenty of time to do it when I get back from Jenny's," Terry reassured her father. Trying to keep his anger under control, Jack responded as calmly as he could, "You violated our agreement. You're not going anywhere, young lady, not tonight, not for a long time." Terry shot back, "I did not. I've still got plenty of time to do my work. I knew it. You don't trust me. You never did. It was a setup like always." Realizing communication was deteriorating, Jack replied in his most carefully clipped tone, "I'm not going to argue with you. Now go to your room before I say something I'll regret." In her most dramatic fashion, close to tears, Terry lamented, "You don't regret that you're making me break my promise to Jenny. She's counting on me, you know." At this point Scott started laughing as he taunted his sister, "Poor Jenny, I'll bet she has another boyfriend problem that only my all-knowing sister the great Terry can help her solve." Feeling ambushed, Terry attacked back, "What would you know about, it you dork? You've never even had a date." Sensing that things were rapidly spinning out of control, Claire intervened, "Enough. Both of you go to your rooms and get busy with your schoolwork right now." Still holding out hope, Scott in his most plaintive voice said, "But I told Roger I'd play Commando with him." "You heard me. Now march." Jack added, "If I find you on the phone or the computer, I'll remove it from your room and you won't get it back for a long, long time." Understandably, *all* the Daleys felt crushed and defeated.

When the elder Daleys finished telling me about their weekend, they were full of questions. What had gone wrong? Were their teens just too immature for them to use authoritative parenting? Were their kids incapable of keeping promises? Would they grow up to be irresponsible? Was there any hope for improvement or should they just resign themselves to constant conflict and rancor? I reassured them that there was hope and that their fears about their children growing into irresponsible adults were ill founded.

Like most parents, the Daleys were well meaning and wanted to be good parents, but lacked a specific plan of action that would help them translate authoritative parenting into a day-by-day routine. To help them bring authoritative parenting to life, I suggested we work together as I taught them step-by-step how to develop and negotiate a positive-behavior contract with their teens. As a first step I recommended they redirect their attention to Terry and Scott's good behaviors.

It's a good idea for every parent with teenagers to make an extra effort to focus on the positive. The next chapter has some practical tips on how to spot the good things your teen does.

2

Focusing on the Positive

As you think about how you parent, you may be surprised to discover that you've gotten into the habit of noticing only the things that your teen does wrong and criticizing him for them. Considering the frustrations of raising teens, this is an easy habit to fall into. While understandable, this pattern of negative attention unfortunately makes matters worse. Teens begin to feel they can't do anything right. They tire of hearing only complaints from their parents and begin to tune them out. Parents get more frustrated and angry as their efforts to "shape up" their teen fall on deaf ears. Behavior and communication continue to deteriorate. In the meantime, teens seek positive attention and support from other, often undesirable, sources. So how do you turn this negative situation around?

Look for Good Behaviors

Your first step is to size up your teen's good behaviors. By good behaviors I mean *anything* positive your teen does that you like—no matter how insignificant or trivial it may seem. Good behaviors can be following the rules you've established for your teen—rules that apply to school, safety, and family life. Good behaviors may include acting responsibly in any capacity. For example, following through on routine behaviors like getting up on time in the morning, being civil to family members, going to school, doing schoolwork, performing chores, coming home on time, calling in when late, and helping out when asked are good behaviors that require some measure of responsibility. While these may seem simple and ordinary—stuff you *expect* from your teen—these daily routine behaviors are the best place to *begin* as you work on helping your teen gain competence and accountability.

Many of my clients are skeptical when I suggest they "accentuate the positive" because it flies in the face of their long-held belief that the best way to decrease irresponsibility and other unwanted behaviors is to create effective punishments. More than 25 years of clinical experience have convinced me of just the opposite. Unless parents begin by concentrating on good behavior, they are wasting their time and may even alienate their teen further. Unfortunately, in families where parents and teens are caught in a negative downward spiral characterized by constant arguments and confrontations, good behavior may be in short supply. Nonetheless it's critical that you spend at least a few days actively looking for good behavior no matter how futile the task may seem.

Go ahead, challenge yourself. Remember *any kind* of good behavior will do. When looking for good behaviors such as taking responsibility and following through, keep the following guidelines in mind:

- **Good behavior is rarely perfect behavior.** When your teen puts forth effort and tries, *that* is good behavior. Your teen doesn't need to get straight As, play a varsity sport, and always act charming to get recognition for good behavior. If she gets up in the morning, goes to school, and/or helps out occasionally, that's good behavior.

- **Good behavior doesn't have to be a monumental achievement.** Of course we'd like our teens to excel at everything, but that's hardly realistic. Look for little things your teen does well. Is he nice to his siblings? Does he finish his schoolwork? Does he let you know where he's going? These are all good behaviors.

- **Good behavior may not happen frequently.** Teens are known for surprising their parents in both positive and negative ways. If out of nowhere your daughter who is an expert dawdler starts getting up and getting ready on Monday and Thursday because she has an early club she likes, that's good behavior—even though she may still be slow as molasses the other days of the week. If your teenage son is habitually late coming home, but for some reason arrives home on time occasionally, that's good behavior.

To Do

Look for good behaviors. Using the guidelines you just read about, make an extra effort to look for things your teen does that you like. You'll be building on these good behaviors when you develop the rules of your contract. If you don't see much that you like, don't worry; a contract can still work.

- **Good behavior can be easy to miss.** Taking responsibility and doing what one is supposed to do often occur quietly without fanfare. If your daughter studies in her room, goes about her business, and doesn't cause a fuss very often, that's good behavior; in fact, that's *great* behavior.

After you've watched your teen for a few days, you should have a pretty good idea of where she stands in terms of good behaviors. Many parents are pleasantly surprised by all the good things their teen is doing that they hadn't noticed until they started focussing on the positive. That was the case with Claire and Jack Daley.

After watching their teens for a few days, the Daleys reported that both Terry and Scott went to school without a problem and were good students although their parents felt they could do better. Both also usually came home on time. Terry was much better about calling in. Scott forgot most of the time. Terry was better at getting up in the morning and keeping her room in manageable order. But Scott was more civil and cooperative—especially at mealtimes and when asked to do chores. All in all Claire and Jack felt hopeful and ready to tackle the next step in making up their behavior contract.

Hopefully you'll be as pleasantly surprised as my clients were. Usually if parents look hard enough they can find at least one little good thing their teen does. However, if after checking things out you discover the grim reality that things are not going well, don't give up hope. In most cases, no matter how bad things are, a contract can help. But bear in mind that, in general, the worse the situation, the longer the contract will take to get things back to normal.

Although you may have noticed some good behaviors, if your relationship with your teen is riddled with zingers (you know—those words and phrases that drive you out of your mind), it can be very hard to focus on the positive things your teen does. If this is the case in your family, the following exercises should help you shift your focus from the negative to the positive.

IDENTIFYING ZINGERS

Many parents find that identifying their teen's zingers greatly improves their ability to concentrate on the positive. By zingers I'm referring to words, phrases, and looks your teen gives you that infuriate you. For example, you may feel zinged when your teen retorts with phrases such as "Make me." "No way." "Yeah, right." "You just don't understand." "You're so unfair." "I hate you."

We parents generally begin most conversations intending to act like the mature rational adults that we are. However, when the battle heats up, our teens can be masters at delivering a zinger that stops us in our tracks, churns up our emotions, accelerates our anger, and reduces us to the developmental age of five or six. Unless we're prepared for this onslaught, we get off track and derail long before we reach our intended destination. Many parents I've worked with have found that a good way to handle this situation is first to identify the words and phrases their teens use that send them over the edge, then practice trading these zingers with a spouse or friend. This approach helps to objectify, depersonalize, and defuse the impact of zingers; in a sense it takes the sting out of the zingers.

To put these steps into action, make a list of what your teen says that really gets to you. You may find that you and your spouse are set off by different things. Don't worry if you're not sure why a particular phrase or gesture sends you out of orbit. Don't be embarrassed about what makes you irrational. The important thing is to identify *what* drives you mad, not *why* it drives you mad. Having identified the culprits, practice trading them with your spouse or a friend. If you need to, look in the mirror and repeat them in a calm, steady tone. As you do this, the absurdity of the statements should become clear, and their power over you should diminish. That's what happened with my clients Sharon and Wayne Williams when they identified and shared their daughter Shana's zingers.

Shana Williams, age 13, was driving her parents batty with her "smart mouth." Whenever Shana disagreed with an opinion or a rule, she got in a dig about how out of touch her mom was. Although Shana varied her phrases, she never failed to hit the age button, e.g., "How could anyone as old as you possibly understand what I'm talking about?" or "My friends all get to take the bus by themselves to the mall. Oh, I forgot you only had horse and buggies when you were growing up. Should I explain what a bus is?" Besides being highly obnoxious, these barbs bothered Sharon because they reminded her of an incident at the supermarket when someone had complimented her on how cute her granddaughter was. Of course there wasn't a granddaughter—it was Shana, her daughter. Sharon's father, Wayne, on the other hand, was nonreactive to age-related remarks. However, he hated it when Shana accused him of not loving her and being selfish. How could she say such hurtful things, he wondered, when deep down she knew he loved her.

After discovering the specific words that really bugged them, Sharon and Wayne started trading them back and forth. At certain points, they couldn't help but laugh as they dramatically delivered Shana's lines. Such an interchange helped reduce the emotional charge of her words and illuminated the absurdity of Shana's statements. Shana's zingers were losing some of their power.

Let me point out that this exercise should not be done with your teen present and is not intended in any way to make fun of your teen. Rather, its goal is to help you deal effectively with disruptive behavior that ultimately can interfere with the success of your contract.

Now that you've identified your teen's zingers, it's time to look at the zingers that we as parents may sometimes use with our teens, such as "Can't you ever do anything right?" "What's the matter with you?" "What were you thinking?" "When are you going to grow up?" Although parents rarely plan to use a verbal bullet with their teens, as their exasperation level climbs, what parent hasn't succumbed to tossing out a zinger or two, e.g., "Don't you remember anything I told you?" "How could you be so irresponsible?" or "I never did anything that stupid as a kid." Often our zingers are in direct response to our teen's zingers. But regardless of who starts a zinger slugfest, mutually exchanged barbs make attempts at compromise, cooperation, and communication impossible.

To help you get your zingers under control, just as you did for your teen, make a list of the zingers you use, share this list with a spouse or friend, and trade them back and forth. Make a note of how it feels to be on the receiving end of your zingers—probably not very good.

As you work thorough the steps of making up your contract, I'd recommend that you try to ignore your teen's zingers. Pay no attention to them. Leave the room when they happen. In addition, I'd strongly suggest that you try to give up *your* zingers. Bite your tongue. Avoid that clever devastating barb you were going to throw. Such restraint may be tough; but as zingers decrease, your job as contract developer and negotiator will be much easier. Because ignoring zingers and stifling the urge to make them yourself is so hard to do, report your efforts to a spouse or friend for support and encouragement.

To Do

Make a list of your teen's zingers as well as your own. Desensitize yourself to their emotional charge by trading them back and forth with your spouse or a friend. And no matter what it takes, try to ignore your teen's zingers and refrain from zinging yourself.

There are a number of additional benefits of decreasing negative, emotionally charged interchanges between you and your kids. Most teens know when they've messed up, and hitting them with a zinger not only is ineffective in producing behavior change, it also is likely to intensify anger and increase the distance between you and your teen. As such hurtful language tapers off, the chances for productive, mutually beneficial communication become more realistic.

Let's switch back to the positive and learn about the importance of positive incentives as a mainstay of your contract.

LEARNING ABOUT INCENTIVES

When you develop your contract, you'll choose incentives to offer your teen for behaving responsibly. Choosing rewards and using them effectively with teens takes finesse and thorough understanding, so please spend extra time on this section to ensure your success.

What Are Incentives?

Incentives are the life breath of behavior contracts. Without them your contract won't work. To acheive the changes you're hoping for, you must reward your teen's good behaviors. There's no way around this. Most teens consider rewards to be such things as participating in activities they like, getting free time at home, and earning credits toward activities or purchases.

Occasionally, parents I work with question the use of rewards, thinking they shouldn't have to "bribe" their teens. I do not consider rewards and bribes to be the same. In the contract you'll be developing, you'll designate rewards as *earned incentives*. You and your teen will *plan out* exactly what he has to do to earn rewards. Earning rewards is like receiving compensation and benefits for a job well done. Do you consider the paycheck you earn a bribe? Or an annual bonus? Most people don't because they've worked to earn their wages. Your teen is earning her incentives by doing her job of acting responsibly, going to school, acquiring skills, and complying with family rules. If you offer your teen money for keeping quiet about something or ask him to lie to help you save face, that's a bribe. A bribe can also take the form of an unplanned present you give your teen for doing something she should do without prompting, e.g., offering your teen a CD if she will return the expensive dress she bought on your credit card without your permission. Bribing your teen to do something he should or shouldn't do is hardly in his best interest and sends a message that you condone deceit. Rewards, on the other hand, when earned, can be empowering for both you and your teen.

As you think about rewards for your teen, keep the following tips in mind:

- **Whatever your teen likes to do or have is a potential reward.** Activities and acquisitions are likely to be the mainstay incentives of your contract. Your teen may enjoy spending time at home talking on the phone, playing a computer game, listening to music, or watching television. He may also enjoy after-school activities like clubs or sports. And what teenager can't find something he really wants to do on the weekend? Weekend activities are powerful rewards. While parents and teens may disagree about the appropriateness of many rewards such as late curfew, exclusive dating, or free use of the car, there are many more they usually can agree on. And what teen would turn down the opportunity to earn credits toward future purchases?

- **Age affects reward preference and suitability.** Of course the age of your teen will influence what rewards are appropriate. Obviously, borrowing the car to go to the movies with a friend may be a good reward for a 17-year-old but is an inappropriate reward for a 14- or 15-year-old. Whatever the age of your teen, and no matter what other parents do, you should never use a reward you object to or are uncomfortable with.

- **Different teenagers may like different things.** Since no two teenagers are alike, make sure you're picking rewards your teen actually likes, not just ones you think she should like. While one teen may consider tickets to the ballet a reward, another may view them as a punishment. The same is true of almost any kind of entertainment or activity; some teens will like it while others won't.

- **Your support and encouragement are two important rewards.** Even though your teen may sometimes act as though he doesn't care about your praise and support, he does. Even if previous attempts to be positive and encouraging have fallen flat, try again. When paired with a positive behavior contract, your kind words will carry more meaning and sincerity.

Your nice words carry enormous weight. Make it a point to recognize and acknowledge your teen's efforts whenever

To Do

Look for activities and stuff your teen enjoys and/or wants. Make it a point to keep an eye out for activities your teen seems to enjoy as well as those she requests. And of course take note of all the things she tells you that she just can't live without. When you make up the contract you'll be including these things and activities as long as you approve of them as rewards.

possible. Even though she may not let you know, it means a lot to her when you voice your care and concern or thanks and appreciation.

Guidelines for Using Incentives

For rewards to work, they must be used according to some very specific, research-based rules. The basics of rewarding are as follows: Rewards must come *after* the behavior; must be earned and not given away; and must be presented positively and consistently, not paired with criticism or punishment. These rules may sound simple enough, but putting them into action can be anything but easy. Let's consider each guideline more specifically.

- **Rewards must come after the good behavior, never before.** As tempting as it may be, don't reward promises of good behavior. Don't cave in—even to heartfelt promises such as, "If you'll just let me go to the movie, I promise I'll do my homework when I get home." Continue to hold your ground as your teen continues with, "But it will be too late to see the movie if I have to do my homework first." Your teen is likely to be correct about this; however, that does not mean she should get to go to the movie. You might suggest she go to the movie over the weekend when she has more time and then talk to her about something she might enjoy doing at home once she finishes her homework.

- **Rewards must be earned.** It's critical that your teen experience the relationship between his behavior and the consequences for that behavior. Rewards or incentives that are earned help your teen learn the cause-and-effect relationship between what he does and what happens to him. For example, if your teen comes home on time, he may be rewarded with the continuing privilege of going out, and eventually he may even earn an extended curfew. On the other hand, if your teen comes home late, the consequence may be that he doesn't get to go out for a night or two. As a first step in taking responsibility for himself and his actions, it is essential that your teen learn the connection between the behavior he does and the consequences he receives. Again, your contract will provide him with continuous opportunities to experience this link. If you get in the habit of giving your teen rewards for no particular reason, the link between cause and effect is lost. Although occasionally it's OK and even fun to give a reward out of the blue, doing so on a regular basis is counterproductive. It teaches your teen that his actions don't really matter and it also gives you too much arbitrary control over your teen, because under these conditions it's totally up to you, not your teen, when he receives a reward.

- **Rewards must be presented positively.** No matter how great the rewards you and your teen come up with, if you don't present them in a positive manner, much of their beneficial effect will be lost. For example, if your son earns the right to play a video game for 30 minutes because he's finished his schoolwork, don't come into his room and disapprove of his reward. Don't say something like, "I wish you wouldn't play that game so much; why don't you do something constructive with your free time?" It's *his* free time; that's the whole point. If his contract includes playing video games as a reward, let him do so in peace. If you don't approve of certain games or activities, don't make them rewards. The same can be said for phone time. Teenagers love the phone, especially most girls. It's a great and safe way to talk about anything and everything. If your daughter has earned free time and chooses to talk on the phone to a friend, that's her choice. Refrain from comments like, "How can you waste so much time on the phone?"

- **Don't mix rewards with criticism.** Pairing praise with criticism is usually demotivating and is likely to cause your teen to view you with suspicion. When you are being positive and supportive, your teen may fear that a criticism or suggestion for change is next on your agenda. For example, say your daughter brings home a test with a grade of B+, and you tell her how proud you are. Don't follow this up with a comment such as "If you studied harder do you think you could get an A next time? You know how important grades are to getting into college." Instead, give your teen your support for a job well done and leave the suggestions about next time until later. If you pair praise with criticism, you're likely to turn your teen off.

- **Practice being positive.** As a way to get back in the habit of being positive, make it a point to say something positive to each family member, your teen included, every day. For example, if the morning routine goes well, not perfectly but nicely, you might comment on how much you appreciate your daughter's cooperation. You could say something like, "Wow, this morning went great. Hope you have a good day at school." You should *not* say, "It's about time you shaped up in the morning. I'm sick to death of your negative attitude." If your son comes home from school on time and calls you at work, let him know how much you appreciate his thoughtfulness. Thank him for remembering to call you and let him know you're looking forward to seeing him when

To Do

Practice being positive. Using the guidelines you just reviewed, say at least one positive thing to your teen every day. If you need to practice being positive, go ahead. You may want to look in the mirror and practice phrases that communicate your positive feelings. Even if you're not accustomed to being positive, try to change. Be yourself, but be positive. In the long run, it's well worth the effort.

you get home from work. Leave it at that. Don't add, "Do you think this newfound responsibility will last until tomorrow or is today it?" If your daughter helps you out by watching her younger brother, thank her for her help. Don't qualify her performance with, "Your brother was so good today it wasn't really a test of whether you've changed." In other words, keep it short, to the point, and, above all else, strictly positive.

Congratulations! You know the foundations of creating a more peaceful home. It's time to begin the next chapter and learn how to translate these fundamentals into a contract format.

PART II

DEVELOPING A CONTRACT

3

Choosing Rules

As you work through this section and decide on the rules, rewards, and discipline methods you want to include in your contract, keep the following guidelines in mind.

Contracts should be a team effort, not an us-against-them situation. Contracts are not meant as devices to catch your teen being bad; rather they should encourage your teen to act better. Contracts are not meant as an impossible mission for your teen. Your contract should include applicable, realistic behaviors. Contracts aren't used to trip your teen up. For example, at the first slip-up you don't offer a recrimination such as, "I knew you'd never be able to follow this contract because you're so immature and irresponsible, you're grounded forever or until you grow up." (Which in this kind of home situation may mean forever.)

A contract is not just a negative-based system in which your teen starts off being allowed to do things and then is punished for goofing up. Contracts must have a positive component. A successful contract provides teens with incentives for doing things you want them to do. If your teen performs certain good behaviors, he earns the privilege of picking something he wants to do. Teens need contracts that include positive incentives to help them learn that their behavior matters and that, within the limits of the contract, by controlling their behavior they can exert control over the consequences that occur. Over time, positive contracts encourage the development of self-monitoring and self-responsibility—skills that benefit each and every teen. Contracts can also create an environment of cooperation that engenders trust and respect.

Although each family comes up with its own set of rules, the set included on the Contract Rule Checklist that follows provides a good starting point. This checklist is a pared-down, bottom-line look at behaviors most parents insist on. It includes what I call must-do and sanity-saver behaviors. Must-do behaviors are behaviors parents should insist on—school-related behaviors, such as attending school and completing schoolwork, and safety-related behaviors, such as asking permission to go out, informing parents of the intended destination, and coming home on time. These behaviors *must* happen so that your teen can acquire the needed skills for becoming an independent, responsible functioning adult. Sanity-savers are behaviors that make life run more smoothly, such as getting up on time, being civil to family members, and helping out when asked. You'll find another copy of this checklist in Appendix A.

Here are some things to think about as you fill out the Contract Rule Checklist.

Safety Rules

This category of must-do behaviors involves safety issues and your peace of mind. Parents need to know their teen is safe.

Contract Rule Checklist

Instructions: Check the rules you want to include in your teen's contract. You can use the space next to each rule to define the rule more specifically.

Safety Rules

- ☐ Give advance notice of plans.
- ☐ Check in.
- ☐ Keep curfew.
- ☐ Engage in agreed-upon activities:

  _____

  _____

  _____

  _____

- ☐ Other rules:

  _____

  _____

School Rules

- ☐ Be on time.
- ☐ Attend all classes.
- ☐ Behave appropriately.
- ☐ Complete assignments on time.
- ☐ Get passing grades.
- ☐ Other rules:

  _____

  _____

Family Rules

- ☐ Get up and ready in the morning.
- ☐ Maintain room.
- ☐ Do other chores.
- ☐ Get along with family members (parents and siblings).
- ☐ Follow through.
- ☐ Behave nicely at mealtimes.
- ☐ Comply with bedtime schedule.
- ☐ Other rules:

  _____

  _____

To Do

Copy: Make a copy of the Contract Rule Checklist in Appendix A.

Fill out: As you review the following safety, school, and family rules, check off the ones that are right for your family and add your own as necessary. As you read through the following descriptions, try to define each rule as specifically and clearly as possible.

Save: Save this checklist—you'll need it when you draft your contract.

Don't be ashamed or embarrassed that you want to know what your teen is up to when he's not home. He lives under your roof and it's not too much to ask that he keep you apprised of his activities. But he may need some encouragement to help him remember to let you know ahead of time where he's going and with whom, to check in (especially if he's going to be late), and to meet his curfew time. Using a contract can help your teen learn these self-responsibility skills in a positive and empowering way. When you negotiate with your teen, you will map out the exact parameters of these safety must-do's, but for now it's a good idea to develop an idea of what you want to include.

- **Give advance notice of plans.** Your teen needs to tell you ahead of time where she's going, with whom, and what she intends to do. Teens seem to change their minds about what they'll be doing from hour to hour; try to be open to last-minute changes. As long as you approve of the activity, try to go along with it. Avoid challenging statements such as, "How come you keep changing your mind? Can't you stick with one thing?" Instead, voice your appreciation that you're being let in on what's going on.

In my family it seemed as though no sooner had one plan been agreed upon than another was hatched. When my sons were in middle school, going to a movie changed to going to the mall, which became going to a friend's house, which morphed into inviting friends over, all in an afternoon's time. While this is frustrating to parents, it's important to take these changes with a grain of salt. Your teen is learning how to plan and organize an event while trying to accommodate a number of different people at the same time. So no matter how frustrating it may seem, hang in there, be happy you're not being shut out, and be sure to let your teen know how much you appreciate being filled in on what's happening.

- **Check in.** Your teen needs to call in when he's supposed to. If no parent is home when your teen comes home from school, insist that she check in with you. If you have a younger teen, find a structured after-school activity for him, as unsupervised time from 3 P.M. to 6 P.M. is when most teens get in trouble. If your teen has a busy schedule, you may ask him to call in to keep you informed of where he is and what he's doing in the morning before he leaves for school. When your teen does check in, always let him know how much you appreciate his call. Do not take this opportunity to interrogate him about his day. Rather, say something nice such as how you're looking forward to getting home and sharing the day. If he's upset when you talk to him, try not to overreact but rather listen, offer support, and let him know that you'll be available to talk more when you get home.

- **Keep curfew.** Your teen should come home on time
  and call in if she's going to be late. You need to set
  both a weekend and a weeknight curfew time.
  Although ultimately these curfew times are your decision, it can be helpful to poll other parents to get an
  idea of when they expect their teens to be home. Start
  with a time you can live with for now. Be prepared in
  the future to consider extending the time if your teen
  shows you responsibility by keeping curfew. This is particularly true for older teens; they are likely to view an
  extended curfew as a sign of your respect and trust.

- **Engage in mutually agreed-upon activities.** Given your
  child's age, his level of responsibility, and your value
  system, what activities can you agree to? In other
  words, what are your ground rules for acceptable
  behavior? Most parents don't allow their teens to
  smoke, drink, or take drugs regardless of their age.
  Most parents don't condone lying. Certainly any kind
  of illegal behavior such as stealing is forbidden as well.
  Behavior that violates the rights of self or other is
  unacceptable.

  You may be concerned about the kinds of movies
  your teen can see. However, because movies are rated,
  your teen is already restricted from seeing certain kinds
  of movies, so you may not need a rule here unless those
  ratings are not well enforced in your area. While most
  teens love parties, those parties without adult supervision should be off limits. I'm not a big fan of teens of
  any age going to unsupervised parties because of the
  inherent risks involved. In my community, someone
  always seems to get into trouble at unchaperoned parties, whether it's driving drunk, getting arrested, or getting beaten up by outsiders. However, these parties
  happen all the time, especially for teens who can drive.

If you have an older responsible teen you may want to be realistic and talk about how he can best handle the situation should he find himself at an unsupervised party. Talk it out and be sure to listen to his views on the best thing to do.

Try to avoid dictating who your teen can have as friends. Instead, take a proactive stance and make it a point to meet all your teen's friends. Invite them over to the house, introduce yourself, and show interest. After that, leave them alone but be quietly available and check in from time to time to see if anyone wants anything to eat or drink. Unless you have evidence that one of your teen's friends is a criminal, don't restrict teen friendships.

Rules about dating will vary depending on the age and maturity level of your teen. Generally speaking, young teens do things in same-sex groups, eventually graduating to mixed-gender groups. Although many young teens date, I discourage this—especially in the case of younger girls dating older boys. Too often in this situation, the girl is pressured into sexual behavior she's not ready for and doesn't understand. A two-year age difference should be the maximum allowed. One-on-one dating certainly can wait until the sophomore or junior year of high school. Never push your teen into dating. There's no rush. After all, he has the rest of his life to be driven crazy by the ups and downs of falling in love.

What are your rules about sexual behavior? For younger teens you can monitor situations in which the opportunity for sexual behavior exists. For older teens, prohibiting sexual behavior and/or trying to monitor it is very difficult, not to mention futile, in most cases. Your best bet is to help your teen develop her own high standards concerning sexual behavior. We'll explore this process in a later chapter that deals with values clarification.

Within the context of your contract, when your teen engages in approved activities, she is not only following rules, she is also enjoying participating in activities that are rewarding in themselves. In other words, if your teen follows the rules of the contract, he earns privileges such as going out and doing the things he wants to do. These activities also serve as rewards; we'll look again at them in the next chapter.

- **Follow other safety rules.** Are there any other safety rules you feel your teen *must* follow? Pick these carefully and don't include very many. Before you decide that any of these behaviors is a must-do, think long and hard. Teens are likely to rebel if you load them up with too many must-do's.

School Rules

Your teen must acquire skills she'll need as an adult. Without a high school education her available choices for the future are severely restricted. I consider going to school and graduating from high school as nonnegotiable must-do behaviors. If college is a possibility, I recommend you strongly encourage your teen to pursue a post–high school degree as well. Complying with a set of school rules helps ensure that she will gain competence from going to school.

At a bare minimum, school rules should include being on time, attending all classes, behaving appropriately, completing assignments on time, and getting passing grades. For younger teens in middle school, making these five conditions part of your contract encourages attention to academics. Even if your teen has no problems in these areas, you may want to include this category as a means of communicating the importance of school rules. However, older self-reliant teens who already comply with these rules and do well in school may not need them specifically included in their contract. Doing well may be rewarding enough. Whatever your teen's situation, don't quit giving occasional words of appreciation, as even the best student enjoys positive feedback.

- **Get to school on time.** Certainly if your teen is tardy once or twice a month and/or gets into minor trouble every so often, a contract that rewards being on time and staying out of trouble may be very beneficial. However, if your teen is tardy frequently, sometimes ditches school, and/or is considered a behavior problem by the school, a contract alone probably will not be enough. The same may be true if your teen frequently gets failing grades. In either situation, I'd recommend talking with your teen's counselor as a first step to getting outside professional help.

- **Attend all classes.** Make sure you're aware of what classes your teen must attend. If this is a problem area, you should ask for the school's help to monitor your teen's attendance.

- **Stay out of trouble.** You should also decide what you mean by the word *misbehavior*. If your teen does something for which the school punishes him with detention, do you consider detention punishment enough, or do you want to add a punishment in his contract? I'd recommend that if detention doesn't seem effective at changing his behavior, you should add a punishment in the contract. Sometimes a double dose helps a teen shape up. If completing assignments and/or getting passing grades is a problem, you may need to come up with a system that involves a teacher's signature to prove acceptable performance in each subject on a weekly basis. Again, see if your teen can comply with these terms of the contract before coming up with stricter ways to monitor her behavior.

- **Finish schoolwork.** A contract can be used to motivate teens, especially younger teens, to do their schoolwork. Starting middle school or junior high brings many new experiences including different teachers and classrooms, more difficult courses, and less structure. A contract that rewards good study habits and completion of work can help your teen get off on the right foot and adapt to these changes. For example, earning free time for completing a certain chunk of work or for studying for a certain time period is usually an effective reward. If your teen has difficulty remembering to bring work home or take it back, you may want to reward this as well, at least until it becomes a habit.

- **Avoid last-minute frenzies.** Planning ahead, e.g., working on reports, writing papers, and studying for a test in a timely manner, should be rewarded. Unlike elementary school teachers, middle school teachers don't remind their students over and over again about assignments that are due. You may want to include a reward when your teens lets you know about upcoming reports and tests.

- **Get passing grades.** Make it a provision that your teen shows you all assignments, tests, and reports on which he is graded. If he fails to do this, work out a system with his teachers. As this is likely to be embarrassing for your teen, don't take this action unless necessary. You might say, "I really hope we can work this out on our own, but if we can't, I'm going to school to talk to your counselor and each of your teachers for their ideas."

- **Obey school rules.** Again, pick only those that are absolutely necessary as too many rules will turn your teen off and thwart your efforts and your contract.

FAMILY RULES

Family rules include sanity-savers. As you think about your family's daily routine, you'll probably identify at least some of the following sanity-savers you'd like to include in your contract. When thinking about family rules, keep expectations low and make the sanity-saver behaviors you select at least initially relatively easy to do.

- **Gets up and off to school without war breaking out.** This means that your teen wakes up on time, gets ready for school on her own, completes any necessary duties, and gets off to school on time. Have a general idea about the time by which your teen needs to get up, what she needs to do to get ready, and when she must leave for school.

  For me, starting the day with everyone trying their best to get up, get ready, and get off to school is worth a great deal. It's something I'm always willing to include as part of a contract. In contrast, starting the day on a negative note filled with begging and threatening can set the stage for a crummy day all the way around. To encourage a morning that "works," you need to think through what needs to be done and approximately how long it takes to do all the activities involved. Based on this estimate along with when your teen needs to be at school, come up with a realistic time for both getting up and leaving for school.

- **Maintain room.** A teen's room is his castle. Still, you may want to ensure that bacteria and mold do not take hold of that sacred space. A contract can help ensure that minimum standards are met. Ask yourself, "What is the least I can live with?" Removal of petrifying food, placement of dirty clothes in the hamper, and return of borrowed items within a certain time period may come to mind. Consider setting a time each day when these standards must be met, perhaps late afternoon or early evening. If you're a neatnik and your teen isn't, ask him to keep his door closed and don't go overboard on your requirements. When you think about it, how much does the condition of your teen's room matter? Teens need venues to express themselves. A teen's room is a safe space to make a statement about who he is at any particular moment. In fact, saving up to buy decorative items for one's room is a desirable reward for many teens.

Decide on a bare minimum your teen could do if he put his mind to it. Then decide on a daily deadline by which she must have maintenance completed.

- **Do chores.** Chores vary considerably between households. You may want to include washing clothes, putting away clothes, washing dishes, helping with food preparation, caring for dogs and cats (feeding, walking, and cleaning up afterward), taking out the trash, cleaning bathrooms, and complying with requests to pitch in and help out. Just make sure you don't require so many chores that your teen has no time to finish schoolwork or enjoy a few minutes to himself.

- **Get along with family members.** Although monosyllabic, barely audible answers may seem the norm for younger teens, especially boys, it won't always be so. As they grow older, miraculously they regain their desire to speak. And certainly teens should be allowed to speak their minds and challenge other people's viewpoints, their parents' included. But no matter what the age, excessive teasing, name calling, fighting, or other nasty behavior shouldn't be allowed. I suggest that you include a rule about being civil to family members as a means of discouraging rude behavior. Family standards will, of course, vary considerably.

- **Follow through.** This is a general category that involves acting responsibly—behaviors such as getting up and ready on his own or going to bed without you reminding him. You may want to add following through on promises or obligations and helping out when asked.

- **Behave nicely at mealtimes.** When the family eats together, your teen should be civil and display acceptable table manners. Decide on your minimum standards for compliance.

- **Comply with bedtime schedule.** For younger teens, set a reasonable bedtime and clarify what your teen needs to accomplish to get ready for bed. Many older teens like to set their own bedtime. If they are able to come home on time and complete what they need to do, this plan should work well. If they can't do this, you may need to set a bedtime for them as well until they've shown they can be responsible in this area.

- **Follow family rules.** Perhaps your teen has one or two quirks that drive you mad because they seem so thoughtless and inconsiderate. For example, if your teen throws down her backpack so that it blocks the front door and makes entering the house comparable to Marine hazard exercises, you may want to include putting her backpack in her room as part of your contract. If your teen dumps his bike in the center of the driveway, causing you to stop the car, get out, and move it in order to get into the garage, include a rule about putting his bike away in your contract. If your daughter always leaves the gas tank empty, you may want to use your contract to help her break this habit. Don't include too many quirks at one time, and, as always, place sanctions only on those that you just can't live with.

The safety, school, and family rules you've just reviewed were chosen because they involve behaviors that are critical to your peace of mind and your teen's future success. As I'm sure you noticed, I did not include rules governing personal tastes or likes and dislikes such as music, clothes, and appearance. While these behaviors may be annoying, in my opinion they represent battles not worth fighting. For example, your teen's school has no doubt already set standards for dress and appearance— why not let the school rules dictate this area? In general, rather than setting up futile, nonworkable rules, I suggest that you try to ignore typical irritating teenage behaviors and preferences related to music, clothes, slang, and the opinions they may have on things they know nothing about. And by all means don't waste your words criticizing them, as this only serves to make these behaviors and preferences more fun for your teen. In fact, I'd recommend that you try to talk with your teen in a non-judgmental way about tastes and interests. Such a conversation can be very illuminating.

Once you've checked off the rules you want to include in your contract, it's time to move on and pick the incentives you want to use.

4

Picking Rewards

Having chosen the rules you want to use, it's time to turn your attention to rewards and pick the incentives you want to use in your contract. Occasionally I work with a family that is resistant to the idea of using a contract that includes rewards. Let's take a quick look at the dangers of omitting incentives from your contract.

Sick of begging and pleading with their 14-year-old daughter, Ramona, to get up in the morning so she'd be on time to school, the Garcias decided that they'd instead do nothing and let Ramona take responsibility for being tardy. They hoped that over time the naturally occurring negative consequences of her irresponsible behavior would be enough to change her habit. Her parents assumed that after being tardy several times and being assigned lunchroom cleanup, Ramona would be so embarrassed that she'd make a point of getting to school on time. Not only did Ramona continue to be late to school, but the assistant principal called Elena Garcia at work two or three mornings a week asking where Ramona was—it became obvious that Ramona was coming to school later and later. When I talked to Ramona about this problem, she explained that her parents, who knew how difficult it was for her to get up, had all but abandoned her in the morning. Although she intended to get up, sleeping a little later was so pleasant that she often fell back to sleep. Her first class was so boring she didn't mind missing it and her grades weren't dropping. On days when there was a test, she somehow got there on time. She also confided that whether she was 2 minutes late or 45 minutes late the penalty was the same, lunchroom cleanup or afternoon detention, consequences that she didn't mind that much. When the assistant principal hinted at suspension, she'd shape up for a few days till the threat passed and then begin the cycle of tardiness again. Clearly Ramona had the situation pegged.

Working together with Ramona and her parents, we developed a contract that offered her an incentive for getting to school on time. In her case her reward was getting to take salsa dancing twice a week after school. Her mother also offered to give her a reminder when it was time to get up, but surprisingly that wasn't necessary. Ramona set her alarm and got up on time.

Like most teens, Ramona responded positively to a contract that provided an incentive for following through rather than just a punishment for goofing up.

CHOOSING REWARDS

When picking rewards for your contract, it's a good idea to include a variety of earnable activities. At home, your teen may enjoy talking on the phone, playing video games, or just daydreaming. Away from home, your teen may find satisfaction with structured activities such as sports and clubs, and/or she may prefer less structured activities and hanging out with

To Do

Copy: **Make a copy of the Contract Reward Checklist in Appendix A.**

Fill out: **Put a check beside each reward you approve of for use in your teen's contract. Expect to add to or revise these rewards when you negotiate with your teen.**

Save: **Keep this checklist. You'll be referring to it when you draft your contract.**

friends. And of course your teen will have ideas of her own about activities she'd like to include and—who knows—you may even agree on some of them. You may also want to provide the opportunity for your teen to earn points that she can exchange for credits toward a future activity or purchase or turn in for money. To help you decide on the rewards you want to use, refer to the Contract Reward Checklist on page 48. You'll find another copy in Appendix A.

Let's take a closer look at the rewards on the checklist.

Activities

Teens have all kinds of activities they want to do—activities that run on a continuum from acceptable to totally *un*acceptable. Be prepared for negotiation here. Although this is an area in which you should allow input from your teen, it's a big help to go into negotiations with at least some idea of what you're willing to consider as activity rewards. The following discussion posits some options, but, given the creativity of teens, I've only scratched the surface.

As you're reading about each reward, ask yourself if you'd be willing to include it in your contract. Don't include any reward that makes you uncomfortable. Pick rewards that are easily accessible.

Contract Reward Checklist

Instructions: Check each reward you are willing to include in your teen's contract. Keep in mind that you'll be discussing the specifics of these rewards when you're in contract negotiations with your teen. The blank spaces are included for any additional rewards you or your teen think of during negotiations.

Weekday Rewards

Activities
- ☐ 15 minutes of free time.
- ☐ Talk on the phone.
- ☐ Play computer game.
- ☐ Listen to music.
- ☐ Watch television.
- ☐ _____
- ☐ _____
- ☐ _____
- ☐ _____

After school and/or evening activities
- ☐ _____
- ☐ _____
- ☐ _____

Bedtime
- ☐ Stay up 30 minutes later.
- ☐ _____

Points
- ☐ Turned in for money.
- ☐ As credit toward future activity/purchase.
- ☐ _____

Weekend Rewards

Activities afternoon/evening
- ☐ Go to a friend's house.
- ☐ Have friend(s) over.
- ☐ Go to the mall.
- ☐ See a movie.
- ☐ Shop.
- ☐ Attend a party.
- ☐ Be driven someplace.
- ☐ Drive.
- ☐ Other entertainment events.
- ☐ _____
- ☐ _____
- ☐ Make a purchase.
- ☐ _____
- ☐ _____

Monthly Rewards
- ☐ _____
- ☐ _____

- **Free time.** Teens love free time. They're faced with so many responsibilities and deadlines that it's great when they can just kick back and do whatever they want, whether it's talking on the phone, watching television, listening to music, or playing on the computer. Short periods of free time (15–30 minutes) make good daily rewards. Teens who have a set bedtime often are especially motivated by the opportunity to use earned free time to stay up 30 minutes later.

  Think about at-home free-time activities you can condone as well as those activities you forbid. Be as lenient as you can here; for example, unless you have a good reason to object, let your teen talk to her friends on the phone, listen to the music she prefers, or watch the TV shows she likes. If you're concerned about content, listen to the music or watch the show yourself. If your teen spends time on the computer, be clear about what she can and can't do. All kinds of inappropriate materials are readily accessible over the Internet. Especially with younger teens, it's a good idea to monitor computer behavior regularly.

- **Weekday activities.** After-school or early evening activities that are structured, such as sports or clubs, may be used as rewards. Less structured activities, such as doing something with friends once or twice a week in the afternoon, can also be included as incentives. Providing transportation or allowing your teen to drive to these activities can be effective rewards as well.

- **Weekend activities.** Teens love to go places and do things with friends, especially on the weekends. This is a powerful and highly desired reward. Your teen may want to invite friends over, go to a friend's house, or get involved in an activity with friends. Looking forward to going to a party, a movie, or even shopping at the mall can be very motivating for your teen.

A shopping trip with you or with their friends is a great reward for many teenagers. Driving younger teens places they want to go or allowing older teens to drive themselves can also work well.

- **Monthly activities.** Big-time events such as concerts, plays, or sports events can make good monthly rewards. More expensive purchases also make good monthly rewards. Some teens even save up for several months to purchase a desired item.

Activity Approval Guidelines

The following guidelines should help you to decide what types of activities you're willing to include as incentives. Being familiar with these considerations will also help you when you negotiate over rewards with your teen.

Any activity at home or away from home may or may not be acceptable to you depending on a number of factors including your teen's destination, companions, mode of transportation, duration of activity, and type of activity.

It's a good idea to think through each of these categories in terms of what's OK and what isn't. Although you have the final say, you can always run your ideas by other parents to get an idea of the current standard. That does not mean you have to agree to the current standard, but it *can* help to know what's happening elsewhere. It can also help to find parents who share your views, as you can be mutually supportive.

Before you approve of an activity, it's important to get as much specific information as possible, which means you're going to need to ask questions. Most teenagers can be vague, evasive, or unsure about what exactly it is that they're planning. When you talk to your teen, let her know that you're asking questions because you care about her, not because you don't trust her. Show interest in her plans, but be firm if you can't approve an activity.

Destination. Teens rarely think in terms of whether their destination is safe or not, so it's your job to do research and determine safety issues. While some public places may be safe during the day, they may not be at night. In addition, if your teen is headed to a friend's house, you need to determine whether there will be an adult present to provide supervision if needed, especially for younger teens and/or a party scenario.

Companions. Of course you'll want to know with whom your teen is going. That's a completely reasonable request, especially for younger teens. You're probably most interested in whether they're "good" kids or troublemakers. If you don't know them, make it a point to meet them, invite them to your house, and spend a little time talking with them. Give your teen the benefit of the doubt when it comes to friends. Unless you have a really good reason to forbid your teen from hanging around with a particular group, let him decide on his own who he wants to associate with.

Transportation. Plans for getting to and from are often fraught with last-minute changes. Try to pin down how your teen is getting there and getting home. Ask questions such as "How are you getting there?" "Do you want me to drive?" (If possible always volunteer to drive.) "Is a parent going to drive?" "Do I know them?" "Are you taking the bus?" If your teen is old enough, he may want to drive or have a friend drive.

Duration. You need to know about when your teen is leaving the house and when he is returning. Certainly he must be home by curfew. If he's going to a public place or even a friend's house, begin with a short duration of an hour or two. Let him prove to you that he can handle this short period before you allow him a longer time away from home. If he wants to hang out somewhere for the whole day and has no particular plans, that's often an invitation for trouble.

Activities. When you decided on your rules in the last chapter, you specified those activities you approved of as well as those you didn't. Keep these in mind as you listen to your teen's request to enjoy a party, event, or activity. And try to determine what your teen intends to do. Don't be afraid to ask questions; it's probably the only way you'll find out what your teen is up to.

Let's look at how to combine these factors when making a judgment about whether you'll allow your teen to do something she wants to do.

For example, if your 14-year-old daughter wants to go to the mall on Saturday afternoon with friends, you might ask her what she thinks they'll be doing—perhaps getting something to eat, going shopping, or seeing a movie. Make sure you know how she's getting there and back. And specify how long she can be gone. As always, have a backup plan that allows her to contact you in case of a change and/or if she needs your help for some reason.

Perhaps your 15-year-old son announces that he's got to go to a friend's party on the coming weekend. Your first question should address whether his friend's parents are going to be home. Be forewarned that the stock answer to this question is, "Of course they are." Your teen knows you want to hear an affirmative reply although he may not know if his friend's parents are going to be home. To be safe rather than sorry, tell your teen that you plan to call the parents and find out if they're going to be home, and do it. The parents may be unaware their teen is even planning a party. You may also want to require your teen to stay at the party and not go elsewhere. Although some parents think it's fine for their teens to attend unchaperoned parties and reason that it's good preparation for when they're on their own, I disagree. Even if you trust your teen completely, without adult supervision all kinds of things can happen. The party can be crashed by unfriendly kids. For example, at a recent unsupervised party in my normally safe local community, a group of teenagers from a nearby neighborhood crashed the party, a fight broke out, and one young man was badly hurt.

Given the possible permutations and combinations of the five factors we've just looked at, it's a good idea to take each situation individually and get all the details before making up your mind and deciding if you approve.

Earning Points

Most teenagers are highly motivated by the chance to earn points.

Points can be used as credits toward a future activity or purchase or exchanged for money. Most teenagers love earning points. After all, what teenager doesn't have an endless array of things he *has* to have, events he *must* attend, and/or items he *can't* live without? Some families use a system of both credits and money. Others focus on credits. If your family is on a tight budget and you don't feel you can afford or don't want to include a monetary reward in your teen's contract, you should set up a system in which your teen exchanges points for credits toward activities he wants to do.

As a general rule, the families I work with who are already offering their son or daughter a basic allowance continue giving their teen this weekly sum independent of the contract. As part of the contract they provide their teen with the opportunity to earn points that can be exchanged for credits or money. The value of an earned point is up to you. To decide on the amount a point is worth it's a good idea to consider your teen's age, the number of points she's likely to earn, and what she's doing to earn points. The families I've worked with have chosen from a wide range, anywhere from 5 cents to 25 cents per point. Again, it's your call. I'd recommend you wait to decide on the point value you want to use until after you've drafted your contract and have some idea of the number of potential points your son or daughter can earn each day. As a rule of thumb, the more points your teen can earn, the lower the value of each point should be.

- **Younger teens do better with credits.** If you have younger teens, you may not want them to exchange their points for cash, as they're likely to spend it long before they've saved enough to get what they want. If this is the case with your teen, you might allow him to turn some of his points in for money and exchange the rest for credits toward the purchase of the desired item. Of course, your teen is allowed to change his mind about what he's saving for and probably will. Using a credit-based point system can encourage teens, especially younger teens, to plan ahead and save up rather than spending every dime the minute they earn it.

- **Older teens may prefer money.** When teens are more responsible about money they can earn cash and budget it themselves. Older teens may want cash directly; hopefully, they have developed some capacity to save up. Expect your teen to occasionally regret a purchase, especially an impulse purchase. Consider it a learning experience. However, if your teen *always* blows her money on purchases she later regrets, perhaps you could begin your contract by using mostly credits for the first month or two—to encourage thinking ahead—and then gradually switch to actual money.

- **Points can be accumulated daily and spent on the weekend.** Points can be used weekly to buy clothes, CDs, computer games, and sports gear. Points can be saved up over time and used to buy concert tickets, a much desired piece of clothing (for example, a prom dress or special pair of shoes), and/or a video game. Your teen might want to earn points toward the purchase of her own phone, installation costs, and monthly service charges. Accumulated points can also go toward getting to do a desired activity such as attending a movie, going out for lunch, or seeing a sporting event.

- **Some families match the points their teen earns.** Each family comes up with its own unique formula for determining who pays for what. Some parents match the points their teen has earned if it's a big expense such as car insurance payments, a computer, or a phone. Matching can help a teen earn something more quickly and thus experience the relationship between following the rules and being rewarded. Again, to match or not to match is totally your call.

- **Points must be earned before they can be spent.** When using points as rewards, make sure they've already been earned. Don't advance credits or money for a big purchase; rather, wait until enough points have been accumulated to cover the cost of the item. Certainly a positive aspect of including money and/or credits as rewards is that it provides you with an opportunity for ongoing discussions about how your teen plans to save and/or budget her money, which is great preparation for the future.

- **Don't reward grades with points.** No matter how good or bad a student your teenager is, don't offer points for test scores or semester grades. For example, don't use a system in which your teen gets $10 for each A he earns. Most families who try this system are hoping it will motivate their teen to do better, but often the teen doesn't have the skills necessary to get such high grades. The system can backfire and demotivate the student because he knows he can't succeed. With most students, rewarding small amounts of work and completed work is much more effective than rewarding grades, the end product of a series of behaviors.

There are other reasons for not using points where grades are concerned. Junior high is more rigorous than elementary school, and an A student may find herself a B student even if she is trying just as hard as she ever has. The same relationship usually holds true for high school, as it's much tougher than middle school. In addition, if your teen is taking a difficult course load with honors or advance-placement classes, it's harder for her to maintain an A average. So again, while grades represent the end product of a series of behaviors, in most cases your contract should reward the process of studying, not the result.

- **Keep points financially realistic.** Whatever rewards you choose, be sure they won't strap you financially. If you can't afford certain incentives, you'll resent giving them and send a mixed message to your teen. When you talk with your teen, be realistic about what's possible and what isn't in terms of both activities and extra money.

Choosing a Reward System

Now that you have chosen the rules you want to use and the rewards you're willing to include on your teen's contract, it's time to decide which rewards you want to use for following safety, school, and family rules.

To help you do this, please refer to the Contract Reward System worksheet that follows. You'll find another copy in Appendix A.

Rewards for Following Safety and School Rules

As a parent and a psychologist, I believe school and safety rules *must be followed.*

Offer Highly Desired Activity Rewards. To motivate your teen to follow these safety and school rules, I recommend that you offer much-desired after-school and weekend activities as rewards. I also strongly encourage you to require that your teen follow all of these rules as the *only way* to earn these particular activities. If your teen is complying with the rules, he is by definition acting in a responsible manner. His demonstration of accountability should earn him the right to continue to enjoy the privileges of getting to go out and have fun. There should be a direct correlation here. The only way he can go out and do things is for your teen to show you that he can follow the rules. Over time, if he is able to maintain this level of responsibility, he should earn the right to do more independent responsible activities. On the other hand, if he doesn't comply, he doesn't earn the activity privileges and may receive disciplinary consequences such as an earlier curfew or a day or two of grounding.

To Do

Copy: Make a copy of the **Contract Reward System** form, which you'll find in **Appendix A.**

Fill in: As you review the following guidelines for creating a reward system, fill in the rewards you plan to offer for following the rules.

Save: You'll need this form when you make up your contract.

Contract Reward System

Instructions: Beside each of the contract rules listed below, indicate the type or number of rewards that can be earned.

Following school and safety rules

 = ___ weekday activities
 = ___ weekend activities

These activities will be chosen by you and your teen on a weekly basis.

Schoolwork bonuses

Doing homework for ___ minutes = ___ minutes of free time or ___ points.

Finishing homework = staying up ___ minutes later or ___ points.

Avoiding last-minute frenzy = ___ points.

Following family rules

Getting ready in the morning = ___ point(s).

Maintaining room by ___ P.M. = ___ point(s).

Doing other chores = ___ point(s) per chore.

Getting along with parents in the morning, in the afternoon, at dinnertime, and in the evening = ___ point(s) for each time period.

Getting along with siblings in the morning, in the afternoon, at dinnertime, and in the evening = ___ point(s) for each time period.

Following through = ___ point(s) each time.

Behaving nicely at mealtime = ___ point(s).

Complying with bedtime schedule = ___ point(s).

Other rules

 _____ = _____ point(s).
 _____ = _____ point(s).

Each point = ___ cents.

 = _____ credit(s) toward an activity.
 = _____ credit(s) toward a purchase.

You and your teen will decide together on the activities and purchases that points can earn. The point or credit value of each activity or purchase will be discussed/negotiated by you and your teen.

If your teen has one minor slip-up during the week, such as being 5 minutes late for school or coming home 10 minutes late, you may use a warning and still allow her to enjoy her activities. If these slip-ups become habits, however, I recommend that you restrict activities. In the next chapter we'll look in detail at handling slip-ups and noncompliance.

Decide on a Realistic Number of Weekday and Weekend Activities. It's a good idea to decide on a realistic number of weekday and weekend activities your teen can earn. There are no hard and fast rules concerning the number of activities, but I advise you not overload yourself or your teen. There may be some activities that have a set mandatory weekly schedule, such as sports teams and clubs, in which case you're plugged into a certain number per week. On the other hand, some activities, especially weekend activities, may not have prearranged times and you can be more flexible when setting a limit. Allowing two nonmandatory weekend activities, one daytime, one evening, should be sufficient for younger teens. As your teen gets older and shows you she can handle more activities, you can increase her limit.

Consider Offering Bonuses for Schoolwork. You may also want to offer bonuses to encourage your teen to stay on task as he does his homework, finishes his homework, and plans ahead. For example, for teens who have difficulty sitting down and studying for long periods of time, consider providing them with an incentive for working for short periods of time (15–30 minutes). The time period you choose should be realistic given your teen's ability to concentrate and the amount of work he needs to accomplish. For example, for each 30 minutes of work your teen completes, you might award him 15 minutes of free time. If he has too much schoolwork to allow him to earn that much free time, he could earn credits toward a future purchase instead. Finishing homework could earn a bonus of

30 minutes to stay up later (a good reward for teens who have a set bedtime) or points toward a future activity or purchase. Preparing ahead of time and completing work without last-minute hassles could earn points as well on either a daily or weekly basis—perhaps 2 points daily or 10 points weekly. These points could be saved as credits toward a weekly or monthly reward.

Rewards for Following Family Rules

Now that you have an idea about how you'll be rewarding compliance with safety and school rules, let's turn our attention to family rules. As you remember, in the last chapter you chose the family rules you wanted to include in your contract. Now it's time to decide how you want to reward your teen for following each of those rules.

Use Points as Rewards for Following Family Rules. Many parents reward their teens for following family rules by awarding points. As noted above, using points provides a flexible reward system, as points can be exchanged for money, converted to credits, or used to buy activities. Each family comes up with its own system of how many points each rule is worth. However, the simplest way is to provide one point for each rule followed unless it's a particularly difficult rule for the specific teen to follow. For the tough-to-comply-with rules, they may offer more points. For example, if getting along with family members is tough for your teen, you can offer him one point for being civil in the morning, one for the afternoon, one for dinnertime, and one for the evening. In addition, you can break up getting along into two categories, one covering parents and the other, siblings. Each chore your teen completes could earn one point, as would each instance in which your teen follows through on an obligation or responsibility. Getting up and ready and going to bed on time could earn one point each.

If you have an older self-sufficient teen, you may not need or want to award her a point for each family rule followed. Instead you could provide a weekly reward for a good week such as extra spending money, an extra opportunity to use the car, or another desired privilege.

Determine the Value of Points in Credits and/or Money. Your next step is to decide how much each point is worth. If you're assigning a monetary value, don't make it so high that you'll need a part-time job to finance it. After all, one of your goals is to spend more positive time with your teen, not less. While 50 cents per point is likely to break the bank for a teen who's earning lots of points, 5 cents or even 10 cents per point may fit within your budget. For example, at 5 cents per point, if your teen earns an average of 10 points per day, that's 50 cents per day and $2.50 per week. If he really excels and earns 15 to 20 points per day, then he earns even more. If you're using money, you have the task of weighing the amount that will motivate your teen against how much you can afford.

As you know, you can also award points that can be turned in for credits toward a purchase or an activity. You might devise a system in which earning an average of 10 points per day (50 per week) could be exchanged for a weekend activity and any additional points earned could be saved as credits toward a future purchase. You might agree to pay for a weekly lesson your teen wants to take and/or offer to drive him if you're available. For example, you might suggest that your daughter invite a friend to lunch and a movie or that your son invite a friend over to play a computer game.

The value of credits is up to you of course and will depend in part on the kinds of things your teen wants to buy. As you begin your contract, suggest lower priced items as reward purchases so that your teen only needs to save credits for a week or two before he gets to spend them on the purchase. To a teen unaccustomed to delaying gratification (and as you know, almost all young teens prefer getting things immediately), waiting a month or two before spending his credits is too long. Your teen will lose motivation unless he periodically receives tangible rewards.

Including Rewards Just for You

Your contract will work best if everyone, including you, has rewards to look forward to. Doing anything that's fun, even if it's nothing at all, may make an enjoyable weekday or weekend reward as well. In addition to providing yourself with little rewards, find supportive friends and/or join forces with your spouse. Talk and share your frustrations and concerns with others you respect and trust. If you do this, you'll be more available to your teen and more understanding and flexible.

Do not get carried away and include a reward that involves you going out of town for the weekend without any supervision for your teen. Even if you have the most responsible teen in the world, there are too many things that can go wrong for an adolescent left home alone for the weekend.

To help you choose rewards, I offer the Parent Reward Checklist, which includes easy-to-do rewards parents have enjoyed.

No matter how airtight your contract is and regardless of how great your incentives, it's almost certain that sooner or later your teen will slip up and break a rule. When this happens, you'll need to have fair and reasonable consequences ready to put into action. The next chapter looks at discipline techniques you can use when your teen breaks the rules of the contract.

To Do

Copy: Make a copy of the Parent Reward Checklist that you'll find in Appendix A.

Fill out: Check off or circle the rewards you'd like to have and add any others.

Save: Put your completed list in a safe, easy-to-find place. Let it remind you to reward yourself.

Parent Reward Checklist

Instructions: The following list includes rewards that parents enjoy. Check off/circle those activities and things you'd like to have as rewards. Add any others you might think of.

Daily Rewards

☐ Take a walk, get some exercise.
☐ Watch television, write a letter, talk to a friend, listen to music.
☐ Read a book, look at the newspaper, flip through a magazine.
☐ Use the computer, learn about something new.
☐ Cook, sew, garden.
☐ Work on car, home-improvement project.
☐ Just do nothing for a few moments.
☐ Other.

Weekly Rewards

☐ Try to get away for a few hours, go somewhere, do something.
☐ Go out for dinner, see a movie, go shopping.
☐ Play a sport, go on a long walk.
☐ Do something fun or just do nothing at all.
☐ Other.

5

Deciding on Discipline

Discipline techniques are much more effective when used in conjunction with a positive contract that provides your teen with incentives for following the rules. By reading the first four chapters you'll learn how to pick rules and rewards, which will make your job of disciplinarian much easier. If you flipped to this chapter without reading the first four chapters, I strongly recommend that you turn back to Chapter 1 and read from the beginning.

Of course each teen is different, but all teens need at least some structure and limits. When deciding on what misbehavior to discipline, it's best to pick your battles carefully, choose a limited number of absolute no's, communicate clearly what will and will not be tolerated, and invoke appropriate consequences for infractions.

The good news is that you've already taken a giant step in this direction by developing a reward system that offers your

To Do

Copy: Make a copy of the Contract Discipline Worksheet, which you'll find in Appendix A.

Fill out: As you learn about the discipline techniques described below, fill out your worksheet by including those techniques that you think will work best in your family.

Save: Keep your worksheet. You'll need it when you talk to your teen about his contract.

teen incentives for complying with school, safety, and family rules. This system discourages problem behavior by rewarding behaviors that are the opposite of problem behavior. For example, rewarding coming home on time discourages coming home late. Providing incentives for studying and finishing schoolwork discourages not doing schoolwork. Rewarding your teen for getting along with the family discourages disrespectful, rude behavior in general. Plan to use your reward system in conjunction with the following discipline techniques. *Do not abandon rewards*, no matter what.

DISCIPLINE TECHNIQUES TO USE

Because rewarding the opposite of problem behavior won't always make problem behavior go away, here are some discipline techniques I recommend you consider including as part of your contract. Use the Contract Discipline Worksheet on page 67 to combine the techniques you'll be reading about into a plan of action. You'll find another copy in Appendix A. As a general rule, use ignoring, warnings, and/or withholding of rewards as your first lines of defense. Only when these techniques are ineffective should you consider taking away a privilege, making curfew earlier, or invoking a grounding.

Contract Discipline Worksheet

Instructions: Check each rule listed below that you are concerned your teen may not be able to follow. Make a note of the discipline techniques you plan to use. Remember, whenever possible, use the techniques of ignoring, warnings, and/or withholding a reward before invoking more heavy-duty consequences such as prohibiting an activity, restricting curfew, or grounding your teen.

Not following safety rules

- ☐ Not giving advance notice of plans
- ☐ Not checking in
- ☐ Not keeping curfew
- ☐ Not engaging in agreed-upon activities
- ☐ Not following other rules

Not following school rules

- ☐ Not being on time
- ☐ Not attending all classes
- ☐ Not behaving appropriately
- ☐ Not completing assignments on time
- ☐ Not getting passing grades
- ☐ Not following other rules

Not following family rules

- ☐ Not getting ready in the morning
- ☐ Not maintaining room
- ☐ Not doing chores
- ☐ Not getting along with parents
- ☐ Not getting along with siblings
- ☐ Not following through
- ☐ Not behaving nicely at mealtimes
- ☐ Not complying with bedtime schedule
- ☐ Not following other rules

Ignoring

- **Ignoring discourages zingers.** As you already know, I recommend that you discourage zingers by ignoring them. Recall that a zinger is an emotionally powerful phrase or word your teen uses that incites you to madness. So when your teen tells you that you just don't understand because you're so stupid, instead of demanding an apology you'll never get, try telling your teen that you're going to ignore her until she can speak to you in a positive and civil manner. Again, if you have to, leave the room.

- **Ignoring also works well with irritating typical teenage behaviors.** Try to ignore the music your teen listens to, the clothes she wears, the strange vocabulary she uses, and the opinions she has about things of which she knows nothing. Criticizing these only serves to make them more fun for your teen.

- **Ignoring means not talking with your teen, not giving him dirty looks, and not using body language to communicate your disapproval.** Since ignoring isn't easy to do in many circumstances because the behavior you're trying not to notice is so noticeable, you may want to leave the room or ask your teen to go to his room. Separating from one another can make ignoring much easier.

  When the Ramirez family decided to quit trying to control their daughters' tastes in music, clothes, and hair color, and instead ignored them, each family member experienced a newfound freedom. The parents, Juan and Rosa, no longer needed to serve as clothing inspectors before their daughters, Rachel, 12, and Maria, 15, left for school. They willingly gave up monitoring the music the girls listened to and they were even able to keep their mouths shut about Maria's ever-changing hair color. The girls were ecstatic. No longer did they have to dread the constant inquisitions over how they looked and what they listened to. Rachel and Maria didn't feel on the defensive all the time. Freed of the need to justify themselves, the girls' interactions with their parents became much more positive. In addition, as their parents expressed their curiosity rather than their censure about the latest trend, the girls actually enjoyed sharing their views on body piercing, tattoos, and whatever else came up for discussion. By not expending effort criticizing personal preferences, the whole family had the energy to focus on more important things.

- **Ignoring can also be effective to help your teen decrease repetitive whining, begging, or nagging.** For example, if even after you've told your son that he can't go to the football game because he didn't turn a report in on time, he continues to beg and plead to get to go, you can let him know you're going to ignore him until he stops his broken-record whining. You may even want to leave the room. Instead of trying to reason with him over and over again, consider stating your position and ignoring him until he can behave more maturely.

- **Ignore arguments unless there's verbal or physical abuse.** Try staying out of your teen's arguments whether they're with friends or siblings. I recommend turning a deaf ear to these squabbles because it encourages the squabblers to reach an agreement on their own. However, if you feel that a behavior is heading out of control, especially if physical contact seems imminent, try giving a calm, simple warning to stop.

Give One Warning

- **Giving one warning can be effective when dealing with any minor or first-time offense.** Whether it concerns a safety, school, or family rule, a warning serves to alert your teen that he's heading in the wrong direction. For example, if your teen is late for school one morning, or forgets to complete an assignment for school, you could remind him that another slip-up means he'll lose the privilege he earns for following school rules, e.g., participating in an after-school activity. Concerning safety rules, if your daughter comes home 15 minutes late or forgets to check in with you, you may want to warn her that continuing to do so will lead to an earlier curfew. In terms of family rules, if your teen and his sibling are headed toward a blowup, you can ask them to stop immediately or they'll lose whatever privilege their contract specifies they receive for getting along and acting civil to one another.

- **Use a warning as a reminder.** You can also use a warning to remind your teen of a request you made for him to do something. For example, if you asked your teen to unload the dishwasher and nothing has happened, you could warn him that unless he does it right now he will lose the incentive he could have earned. Warnings should not be threats of dire consequences; they should be specific, calmly delivered requests to stop or start doing something.

- **Using a warning helps your teen to stop and take a look at what he's doing.** You're providing him with practice in monitoring his own behavior. In time, with enough experience, the chances are good that he'll provide his own signal to stop to take a look at what he's doing and to correct it.

Losing Privileges

- **Withhold activities or points that would have been earned for contract compliance.** If a warning isn't enough to turn your teen's behavior around, you should consider depriving her of the desired activity or number of points she would have earned for compliance. For example, if your teen doesn't complete her homework, she loses the privilege of using her free time to stay up later; if your teen can't get up in time in the morning and get to school on time, she loses the privilege of a special after-school activity; if your teen can't interact pleasantly with her younger brother for a few minutes each day, she may lose the privilege of extra free time to herself or the opportunity to earn extra points.

  When the Hubbards came to me, they were desperate. Their 15-year-old daughter, Katie, was always on the phone. Although she always promised she'd get off in "just a minute," the minutes seemed to turn into hours. Katie's mother, Gwen, was especially sick of asking her to get off the phone. Working together, we came up with a plan that specified that only after Katie had finished her homework would she be allowed to talk on the phone. If she got a call, she was allowed one minute to let her friend know she'd call her back. Although Katie much preferred being on the phone to studying, she knew that if she didn't finish her schoolwork, she wouldn't be allowed to use the phone. In addition, if she broke this rule, her phone would be removed and she would be denied phone time for the following two nights. Not wanting to be denied access to the phone helped motivate Katie to finish her schoolwork.

- **Delay the opportunity to enjoy a reward.** If your teen has had a terrible day or week complying with family rules, you may not allow her to cash in her points at the end of the day/week. You don't take her points away from her, but you don't let her spend them until she's able to show you better behavior.

Earlier Curfew

- **If losing privileges, including activities and points, isn't effective in changing a behavior, consider making curfew earlier.** If your teen is no more than 30 minutes late, you might try doubling the number of minutes your teen is late and subtracting these minutes from her curfew time. Using this formula, if your teen's curfew on weeknights is 9 P.M., and she comes home at 9:30 P.M., her curfew for the rest of the week would be 8 P.M. If she's late again, quadruple the minutes and subtract them from her curfew, making her curfew 7 P.M. If she still comes home late, it's time to consider grounding her for at least one night.

Grounding

- **Grounding significantly limits privileges.** Sometimes you need to impose a restriction such as grounding that significantly limits privileges, especially when school or safety rules have been violated. Most parents forbid their teen to use the phone, play video games, or watch television as terms of their grounding. And, of course, friends aren't allowed to visit. Is there anything worse than being confined to one's own home, especially on the weekend? Probably, but most teens can't think of anything worse.

- **Use grounding for short periods of time.** Grounding works best if it is used sparingly and invoked for short periods of time. Too many parents come down with lengthy groundings like confining their teen to home for a week or two. Under such circumstances, teens are likely to become even more obnoxious. As a result, parents may revoke the grounding because they can't stand having their teen around. This lets the teen know that bad behavior *can* lead to her desired outcome—the ability to go out.

- **Use grounding selectively.** Grounding should be saved for serious situations, especially those that involve infractions of school or safety rules. If grounding is overused it will lose its effectiveness. It's easy to get in the habit of relying too heavily on grounding as a discipline technique. This was the case with the Mitchell family.

  When Doris and Ralph Mitchell came to see me, they were feeling what they termed "grounded out." They were constantly struggling with the question, "To ground or not to ground?" Exacerbating the situation, Doris was a self-admitted undergrounder and Ralph was a bona fide overgrounder. Needless to say, their son, Jake, 16, had learned how to manipulate this situation very effectively. For example, recently his father prescribed a month-long grounding because Jake had failed to rake the yard as he had promised and talked back to his dad when confronted. Jake instantly appealed to his mother, citing all the reasons this punishment was unfair. Compounding the confusion, Doris agreed with Jake that his dad had overreacted and eventually caved in to Jake's request to go out that evening. When Ralph discovered that Jake had sneaked out of the house, he threw a fit, castigated his wife, and waited up for Jake's return, ready to come down with an even more severe punishment. Knowing that his father was probably waiting up, Jake called to tell his mom he was staying at a friend's house, hoping his dad would calm down by the next morning.

Meeting with Doris, Ralph, and Jake together, I proposed we develop a contract that provided positive incentives for following the rules, as well as negative consequences, such as grounding for major slip-ups. Once he heard about the possibility of positive rewards, Jake brightened up. Maybe this contract wasn't such a bad idea after all. In addition to the positive aspects, earning credits for following school, safety, and family rules, we outlined violations that were serious enough to merit a one-night weekend grounding, such as coming home more than 30 minutes late. In addition, before a grounding was invoked, Doris and Ralph had to agree that the circumstances called for it. As is typical, Jake tested the terms of the contract. When he came home 45 minutes late, he was sure his mother would understand that he was having such a good time that he didn't notice how late it was. Breaking with tradition, Doris did not fold. She and Ralph let Jake know he had violated the contract and that he would be grounded for the next evening. Once Jake realized that the contract was real, he started behaving much better. Not only did he want to avoid being grounded, he also wanted to earn positive incentives. As a bonus, Jake and his dad weren't at each other's throats nearly as much, which meant Jake's parents weren't undermining each other.

If you find yourself frequently on the verge of grounding, remember the cliché that "you can catch more flies with honey than with vinegar." Think about the situation from a positive perspective. Is there something you can do to encourage better behavior and make grounding less necessary? Of course the answer is yes. In fact, if you're following along with this book, you're already doing it—developing a contract that provides positive incentives for following the rules.

By including these discipline techniques in your contract, your teen will experience the connection between his behavior (breaking the rules) and the consequences (losing a privilege). As this connection becomes ingrained, your teen will start to internalize the relationship. In time, although tempted to come home late, he'll reconsider because he knows he'll lose a privilege for doing so and may even be grounded. Even though sleeping in is pleasant, your daughter will remind herself to set her alarm and get to school on time because she doesn't want to lose a privilege such as an after-school activity.

DISCIPLINE TECHNIQUES *NOT* TO USE

Let's take a look at discipline techniques I strongly urge you *not* to employ. These techniques are ineffective, and they usually make things worse, not better.

No Physical or Verbal Abuse

No matter how angry you are with your teen, avoid using physical punishment. Don't get into a fight or hit your teen. Don't threaten him with violence. And don't emotionally abuse him by berating and intimidating him. Getting tough is usually a last-resort measure, employed by parents who are desperate to get things under control. Although such tactics may seem to work in the short run, don't be fooled. In the long run, using this kind of force is counterproductive and causes many more problems than it solves.

In fact, many problems can intensify and increase when parents use overly severe punishments. Many teens tend to view these attempts as an invitation to engage in a power struggle and thereby up the ante as they strive to prove their will is stronger than their parents'. As the battle escalates, it becomes obvious that no one is the winner. Feelings get hurt and anger intensifies on both sides. Teens may become even more alienated from their parents—and more rebellious.

Certainly as a parent you need to supply consequences when your teen violates the rules of your contract, but again, these consequences should not emotionally and/or physically abuse your teen. If getting tough is an ingrained habit, I recommend that you consider getting counseling to help you manage your anger. In addition, you and your teen might benefit from outside advice on how to relate to each other without blowing up.

Avoid Double Secret Probation

One of the reasons a contract works is because the rules are out in the open, not secret. In the movie *Animal House*, failing grades and atrocious behavior earned the Deltas double secret probation, which, of course, didn't work because it was *secret*. (Not that I'm sure it would have worked under any circumstances with that group of rowdies.) However, the point here is to let your teen know ahead of time about the consequences of violating rules whenever possible. You can't anticipate every situation, but general guidelines help. Your contract starts this process. If your son or daughter really goofs up, however, let him/her know how upset you are and why, and that you're trying to come up with a fair punishment. It is not necessary that your teen agree with you about what is fair.

Repair Overreacting

No matter how calm and collected you usually are, given the ingenuity of your teenager and the stresses of everyday life, you will from time to time overreact. So it's a good idea to have a plan to counteract your slip-ups when you overreact and at the last minute come down with a desperate attempt to control either the uncontrollable or the not really important. Unenforceable and pointless punishments such as excessive grounding or taking away phone privileges for life erode your position of authority and lessen your credibility. In the emotion of the moment, who hasn't blurted out some dire punishment that's way over the top? I know I have.

When you act too hastily, your punishment may have more to do with the mood you're in than the actual infraction or seriousness of the misdeed. You may be responding to the last straw, whether it's your daughter being on the phone, getting home 10 minutes late, teasing her sister, talking back, or leaving her backpack at a friend's house. (These things happen every day!) When you overreact, and it happens to all of us, you need to regroup, apologize, and work together to come up with something more reasonable.

If you find yourself really furious, ready to invoke 15 years to life, take a deep breath and give yourself as much time as you need to determine an appropriate punishment. You can say something such as, "I'm so mad right now I can't think straight. I need to think about what you did and what kind of punishment you've earned. I'll come talk to you when I've calmed down." Giving your teen this kind of message may encourage him to think about what he did and why it was wrong.

Don't Invade Your Teen's Privacy

Unless you have a *well-founded* suspicion of potential harm, illegal activity, or impending incarceration, enforcing discipline rules should *never* involve an invasion of your teen's privacy. In other words, stay out of your teen's room. Do not search through his drawers looking for evidence of wrongdoing unless his behavior gives you reason to do so. Do not read your daughter's diary looking for clues about what she's doing. Talk with her about your concerns. Don't accuse her, rather share that you're not sure what's going on. Listen carefully to her answers. Wait for her to share with you. If you are still suspicious of your teen's behavior, talk with her guidance counselor and consider getting professional psychological help to figure out what's going on. As noted before, the more you can talk with your teen about troublesome areas on an ongoing basis, the better it will be for both you and her.

Don't Attempt to Censor

It's never a good discipline technique to censor information from your teen. Parents may mistakenly think they can shield their teens from temptation and problem behavior by prohibiting access to materials dealing with sex, drugs, alcohol, music, violence, etc. This attempt *never* works. In fact, it often backfires, as prohibition leads to heightened interest. Rather than forbidding these subjects, you need to be available to talk with your teen about the issues that interest him. Your teen needs to feel comfortable talking with you, especially about areas that concern him.

The Robertsons came to me concerned about whether their 14-year-old son, Jon, was at risk for getting into trouble. Jon was the Robertsons' oldest child, and the parents were the first to admit they were unfamiliar with today's teenagers. Almost every article they read was alarmist, suggesting that teens—a troubled immoral rebellious lot—were destined to failure and self-destruction via drugs and sex. This constant barrage of warnings and dangers had turned the Robertsons into vigilant overseers of every aspect of Jon's behavior. Ironically, as a result of their concerns, they stopped acknowledging the good things Jon did and instead tried to censor what he was exposed to. They focused on what they considered possible indicators that Jon was headed for trouble. Did his messy room, his lack of communication, his peculiar clothes, and his taste in music signify disdain for his family and affiliation with the wrong crowd? Should they search his room to make sure he was telling the truth about not being involved in drugs? Could they trust him? The questions plagued them.

Since Jon's previous behavior was far from antisocial or impulsive and since he wasn't displaying any behavior out of the normal range, I felt the Robertsons' concerns were probably unfounded. I suggested we work out a contract that acknowledged and rewarded Jon's good behaviors. After a few weeks of focusing on the positive, Jon's parents were no longer so suspicious and stopped censoring and monitoring his every move. Since Jon experienced his parents becoming more supportive and caring, he started opening up to them and sharing his concerns. In time they talked openly about almost everything, including his concern over the fact that some of his classmates' older brothers and sisters were taking drugs and experimenting with sex.

DISCIPLINE SUMMARY

Here's a summary of a general strategy many parents have found effective to nip problems in the bud and/or prevent them in the future.

- Don't get caught up in a negative net of punishment: It's important that you think through consequences for rule infractions, but with adolescents the trick is to be proactive—to prevent as many problems as possible from happening in the first place; thus decreasing the probability of needing to use discipline as frequently. As you know, that's what a positive-based contract is all about.

- Do use: ignoring, a warning, loss of privileges, earlier curfew, and grounding.

- No matter what, don't use: physical or verbal abuse, double secret probation, overreacting, invasion of privacy, or censorship.

- For not following school rules: Minor violations, such as one tardy or getting a bad grade on a quiz, might get a warning that repetition of the behavior will result in a privilege such as an after-school activity being taken away. If school rules continue to be violated during the week, you should enforce your punishment and eliminate after-school activities.

- For not following safety rules: Again, for a first or minor offense such as coming home 5 to 10 minutes late or forgetting to call home on time, you can issue a warning. Subsequent lapses of memory on your teen's part could be met with an earlier curfew. For example, coming home more than 15 minutes late might earn a 30-minute earlier curfew. Continued inability to arrive home on time could warrant a one-night grounding.

- For not following family rules: A warning can be used to remind your teen of the rule he isn't following. If your warning isn't heeded, you can use a consequence such as not awarding him points and/or restricting such free-time activities as staying up later, talking on the phone, playing a video game, or watching television. If your teen has a bad day/week in terms of following family rules, do not allow him to cash in his points. Store them for him until he's had a better day/week.

In Chapter 13 we'll take a close look at how to deal with more serious and/or recurrent contract violations and when to call in extra outside help. But for now, try to stick with the techniques you just learned about unless your teen is out of control. If this is the case, turn to Chapter 13 on when and how to get extra help.

Now that you have chosen all the components of your contract, it's time to turn to Part III and learn how to pull them all together into a viable contract.

PART III

FINALIZING A VIABLE CONTRACT

6

Selecting Your Contract's Format

The scope and format of your contract will depend on your areas of concern as well as the rules, rewards, and discipline techniques you choose to include. Before you negotiate your contract with your teen, it's a good idea to have a contract document to work from. Your contract document should include written sections covering the following.

- **Rules and rewards.** Certainly your document should contain a list of the rules you expect your teen to follow, the rewards he can earn for following them, and a means of keeping track of the rewards earned and spent.

- **Discipline.** Some parents include a section that lists the discipline techniques that will occur for contract violations. Others do not feel the need to list these in the contract itself, as they consider the discipline worksheet they made up to be sufficient. Of course, you do want to have a discipline plan to put into action if needed; however, by including a written section on discipline as part of your formal contract, you may be sending the message to your teen that you don't trust him and that you expect him to violate the rules. This type of non-empowering message is often unnecessary, and in fact it is generally counterproductive for teens who rarely get in trouble. I suggest that you ask your teen how he feels about a section on discipline being included. On the other hand, if your teen *chronically* gets into trouble, that's another matter. We'll consider how to structure a contract in this circumstance in a later chapter, but be forewarned that a contract alone may not be enough to shape up a chronic offender.

- **A signed and dated statement by your teen.** This statement should indicate that your teen understands and accepts the terms of the contract. For example, "I, (name of teen), agree to follow the rules listed in this contract in return for which I will be compensated as noted."

- **A signed and dated promise by you, the parent.** This statement should indicate that you promise to comply with the terms of the contract. For example, "I, (name of parent), the parent of (name of teen), agree to honor the terms of this contract and provide compensation as noted."

- **A fresh contract form each week.** In most cases, a fresh contract form should be used for each week. Any necessary updates or changes should be made and then the contract should be signed by the teen and the parent.

CONTRACT FORMATS

To help you decide on the contract scope and format that's best for your teen, please review the following formats and take a look at how different families put them into action.

Comprehensive Contract

The first format we're going to review I call the Comprehensive Contract because it is the most detailed. It spells out everything and allows you space to record whether or not each rule is followed on a daily basis. When they begin contracting, many parents especially those with younger teens, use this detailed format—it reminds everyone of what needs to be done and helps parents to be vigilant and keep track of everything their teen does. Even if your teen isn't having difficulty with all of the rules listed on this detailed format, you may want to include them, especially the safety rules. Making these rules part of your contract helps familiarize your teen with them and signals their importance. As your teen gets older and takes on more responsibility, his previous exposure to these rules, especially the safety rules, will make him better able to follow more grown-up rules.

If you have an older teen who is self-sufficient, you may not need to be as specific. Later in this chapter we'll look at a format more suitable for older teens. Keep in mind that, no matter what kind of format you begin with, you can always change it. For example, as your teen improves you may switch from separately logging in compliance with each rule to an overall daily written evaluation and finally to a weekly evaluation.

Let's take a look at the most specific format. Page one, "Comprehensive Contract: Safety and School Rules," provides space for you to record compliance on a daily basis for each safety and school rule followed. There is also a section for listing agreed-upon weekday and weekend activities your teen can choose from. There is another section that covers schoolwork bonuses and rewards.

Page two, "Comprehensive Contract: Family Rules," provides you with a system to keep track of the family rules your teen follows and the points he earns. Using this form, you and your teen can tally up points earned each day and total them at the end of the week. At the bottom of the form is a section in which you indicate the value of points in terms of money or credits toward an activity or purchase.

Using a Comprehensive Contract

Let's see how the Jeffersons, Susan and Ray, used the comprehensive contract format that you just read about with their 13-year-old-son, Joe.

Joe, an eighth-grader at middle school, was having difficulty with schoolwork, especially literature and social studies, because each subject required a great deal of reading. Joe not only procrastinated about getting started with his homework, but he also wasn't able to concentrate on his studies for very long. In addition, Joe complained that he couldn't get his work done because his younger brother Jack wouldn't let him alone. As a result Joe had retaliated by teasing Jack almost nonstop.

Otherwise Joe was doing well. He got to school on time and followed other school rules. Curfew wasn't a problem because he was dependent on his parents or friends' parents to drive him places. His parents found most of the activities he wanted to do acceptable, such as spending time with his good friends

Comprehensive Contract
Safety and School Rules

Safety Rules

	M	T	W	Th	F	Sa	Sun
☐ Give advance notice of plans.							
☐ Check in.							
☐ Keep curfew.							
☐ Engage in agreed-upon activities:							
_____							
_____							
_____							
_____							
☐ Other rules:							
_____							
_____							

School Rules

	M	T	W	Th	F	Sa	Sun
☐ Be on time.							
☐ Attend all classes.							
☐ Behave appropriately.							
☐ Complete assignments on time.							
☐ Get passing grades.							
☐ Other rules:							
_____							
_____							

Complying with all safety and school rules each day earns the privilege of getting to participate in ____ after-school activities and ____ weekend activities. Activities to choose from this week are:

Weekday activities: _____

Weekend activities: _____

Bonuses for complying with the school rules:

Doing schoolwork or spending time reading or learning for ____ minutes = ____ minutes of free time or ____ points.

Finishing schoolwork earns staying up ____ minutes later or ____ points. Preparing ahead of time and completing work without last-minute hassles = ____ points.

I, _____ , agree to follow the rules listed above in return for which I will be compensated as noted.

Signed _____ Date _____

I/We, _____ , the parent(s) of _____ , agree to honor the terms of this contract and provide compensation as noted.

Signed _____ Date _____

Comprehensive Contract
Family Rules

Family Rules

	M	T	W	Th	F	Sa	Sun

☐ Getting ready = ___ pt(s).
☐ Maintaining room = ___ pt(s).
☐ Other chores:

    _____ = pt(s).
    _____ = pt(s).
    _____ = pt(s).

☐ Getting along with parents
    morning   = ____ pt(s).
    afternoon = ____ pt(s).
    dinnertime = ____ pt(s).
    evening   = ____ pt(s).
☐ Getting along with siblings
    morning   = ____ pt(s).
    afternoon = ____ pt(s).
    dinnertime = ____ pt(s).
    evening   = ____ pt(s).
☐ Following through
    = ___ pt(s) each time.
☐ Behaving nicely at mealtimes
    = ___ pt(s).
☐ Complying with bedtime
    schedule = ___ pt(s).
☐ Other rules:

    _____
    _____

Total points earned per day: _____

Total points earned per week: _____

Value of points: 1 point = ___ cents/ ___ credits toward activity/purchase.

Ideas about how to spend points:

    Free time: ___ minutes free time costs ___ points.

    Future activity and cost in credits:

        _____ costs ___ credits.
        _____ costs ___ credits.

    Future purchase and cost in credits:

        _____ costs ___ credits.
        _____ costs ___ credits.

I, _____ , agree to follow the family rules listed above for which I will earn points and be compensated as noted.

Signed _____ Date _____

I/We, _____ , the parent(s) of _____ , agree to honor this contract and comply with its terms.

Signed _____ Date _____

Jerry and Todd playing sports or video games, or just hanging out at each other's houses. Although he followed most family rules, his room, like those of many teenagers, was far from orderly. However, if asked he'd usually make an effort to straighten it up a bit. Given his parents' concerns, we came up with a contract that contained a few provisions.

Because getting Joe to finish his schoolwork was the Jeffersons' biggest concern, we started there. To motivate Joe to do his schoolwork, he could earn 15 minutes of free time for each 30 minutes of studying. Since he had about 90 minutes of schoolwork each night, he could earn 45 minutes of free time. When he completed his schoolwork he earned an additional 30 minutes of free time, which he could use to stay up later.

To encourage Joe to get along better with his brother, he could earn up to 12 points (three each for morning, afternoon, dinnertime, and evening) that were exchangeable for credits toward a future purchase. Joe wanted a new baseball glove that cost $25. Each point he earned was worth 5 cents toward the glove. To sweeten the pot, for each day Joe was able to complete his schoolwork on time, his parents agreed to match the amount that Joe earned that day for getting along with his brother. So, for example, if Joe earned nine points on Monday for getting along with Jack and finished his homework on time, his parents would award him an additional nine points. In addition, the Jeffersons rewarded Joe's younger brother, Jack, for not bugging Joe for an extra bedtime story. This plan provided incentives for both brothers to get along.

Even though the Jeffersons weren't concerned about how well Joe followed the other family, safety, and school rules, they decided to include them as a kind of insurance policy. Sometimes when parents only reward a few of their family rules, their teen falls down on complying with those rules that are left out. Therefore, Susan and Ray decided to reward one point for the remaining family rules as noted below on their contract. They wanted to include school and safety rules, again as insurance.

Comprehensive Contract
Safety and School Rules for Joe Jefferson

Safety Rules

- ☐ Give advance notice of plans.
- ☐ Check in.
- ☐ Keep curfew.
- ☐ Engage in agreed-upon activities.
- _____
- _____
- _____
- _____
- ☐ Other rules:
- _____
- _____

M	T	W	Th	F	Sa	Sun

School Rules

- ☐ Be on time.
- ☐ Attend all classes.
- ☐ Behave appropriately.
- ☐ Complete assignments on time.
- ☐ Get passing grades.
- ☐ Other rules:
- _____
- _____

M	T	W	Th	F	Sa	Sun

Complying with all safety and school rules each day earns the privilege of getting to participate in ____ after-school activities and ____ weekend activities. Activities to choose from this week are:

Weekday activities: _Baseball practice Mon. & Thurs._

Weekend activities: _Weekend fun activity: 3 friends for pizza & video_

Bonuses for complying with the school rules:

Doing schoolwork or spending time reading or learning for _30_ minutes = _15_ minutes free time.

Finishing schoolwork earns staying up _30_ minutes later.

For finishing schoolwork each evening parents will match points earned for getting along with Jack.

I, _Joe Jefferson_ , agree to follow the rules listed above in return for which I will be compensated as noted.

Signed _____Joe Jefferson_____ Date _____

I/We, _Susan & Ray Jefferson_ , the parent(s) of _Joe Jefferson_ , agree to honor the terms of this contract and provide compensation as noted.

Signed _____Susan Jefferson, Ray Jefferson_____ Date _____

Comprehensive Contract
Family Rules for Joe Jefferson

Family Rules

	M	T	W	Th	F	Sa	Sun
☐ Getting ready = 1 pt.							
☐ Maintaining room = 1 pt.							
☐ Other chores:							
feed the dog = 1 pt.							
pack backpack = 1 pt.							
help w/ dinner = 1 pt.							
☐ Getting along with parents							
morning = 1 pt.							
afternoon = 1 pt.							
dinnertime = 1 pt.							
evening =1 pt.							
☐ Getting along with siblings							
morning = 3 pts.							
afternoon = 3 pts.							
dinnertime = 3 pts.							
evening = 3 pts.							
☐ Following through = 1 pt each time.							
☐ Behaving nicely at mealtimes = 1 pt.							
☐ Complying with bedtime schedule = 1 pt.							
☐ Other rules: _____							
_____							

Total points earned per day: _____

Total points earned per week: _____

Value of points: 1 point = 5 cents/ 1 credit toward activity/ 1 credit toward purchase.

Ideas about how to spend points:

  Free time: ____ minutes free time costs ___ points.

  Future activity and cost in credits:

  _____ costs ___ credits.

  _____ costs ___ credits.

  Future purchase and cost in credits:

  _Baseball glove_____ costs _$25 or 500_ credits.

  _____ costs _____ credits.

I, _Joe Jefferson_ , agree to follow the family rules listed above for which I will earn points and be compensated as noted.

Signed _____Joe Jefferson_____ Date _____

I/We, _Susan & Ray Jefferson_ , the parent(s) of _Joe Jefferson_ , agree to honor this contract and comply with its terms.

Signed ____Susan Jefferson, Ray Jefferson____ Date _____

As a reward for following these rules each day, Joe could earn after-school baseball practice, as well as one or two weekend fun activities with his friends. By acknowledging and rewarding Joe's compliance with these rules, his parents were teaching him the connection between acting responsibly and positive consequences. This kind of proactive approach that rewards accountability can only benefit Joe as he grows older and wants to be given more freedom.

Let's look at Joe's contract and how he did the first week.

As expected, Joe was 100 percent on following safety rules. His performance on school rules was good as well. Rewarding Joe for doing small chunks of schoolwork as well as for finishing his homework seemed to motivate Joe and helped him stay on task. Every evening Joe was able to finish his homework on time. Joe was very proud of his performance on both the school and safety rules. He even asked to enter the checkmarks on his contract himself. During the week he went to baseball practice on Monday and Thursday. On the weekend he invited some friends over for pizza and a four-way computer game.

Although Joe had stated very confidently that he'd ace the family rules, he found getting along with his brother, Jack, to be much more difficult than he had anticipated. The first few days were particularly frustrating. He couldn't believe that he didn't get points when not getting along with Jack when the trouble was clearly Jack's fault. "How unfair is that?" he asked his parents, who turned a deaf ear to his protestations. And to add insult to injury, he also lost points for getting along with his parents because he argued so much about whose fault it was that he and Jack weren't getting along.

Realizing that Joe was floundering, his dad decided that Joe could benefit from some coaching to help him deal with Jack's button-pushing behavior. Initially he suggested that Joe leave the room and settle down. Having mastered that skill, Joe next tried warning Jack that he wasn't going to listen until he could say something nice. And finally, hit with the reality that arguing with his parents about Jack's role in their arguments was futile, Joe gave up this tactic. Fortunately for Joe, during the first week he did well following the other family rules and thus earned a decent number of points. By the end of the week Joe had earned 85 points plus 17 matched points from his parents. At that rate, he'd be able to earn his new baseball glove in less than six weeks.

When it was time to make up the next week's contract, in spite of the difficulties Joe had faced, everyone was in agreement to keep the contract the same. We'll check in again with the Jeffersons in a later chapter to see how their contract fared over the first few months.

Advantages of Beginning with a Comprehensive Contract. You can use all or part of the comprehensive format you just learned about. Although it may be tempting to develop a limited contract that covers only those rules your teen is having difficulty following, there can be a definite downside to this approach. Since altering behavior takes time and motivation, a contract that asks for too much immediate change may backfire. Your teen may try to follow the rules but be unable, earn few if any rewards, and thus view his contract as impossible. For example, if your teen is having difficulty with school, improving his study skills is likely to take time—certainly more than a few days or a week. If your teen is characteristically confrontative and argumentative, learning how to get along with parents and/or siblings is likely to be a long road as well. For these reasons I always recommend that your contract include at least several rules your teen is pretty good about following. This inclusion ensures that your teen will be able to earn some incentives and won't lose interest in the contract before he has a realistic chance to improve in the areas that concern you.

With my sons I began by using a comprehensive contract to ensure that they earned at least some rewards for behavior they could already do while improving other behaviors. When they were younger teens I used a very specific format that detailed all the family rules. They were pretty good about following these rules at this point because they had been brought up playing the Behavior Game, a younger child's version of the contract you're learning about (explained in my earlier book, *How to Keep Your Kids from Driving You Crazy*); by including family rules I ensured that my sons would earn at least some rewards. As problems arose, especially those concerning schoolwork, I'd tailor the contract to focus on whatever these difficult areas were. Usually I would provide a special reward for improvement in the targeted categories.

For example, when my older son, Mike, was in seventh grade, we used a contract that focused on planning ahead and getting assignments done on time. These areas of concentration were chosen after I discovered at the first quarter teacher conferences that Mike's grades were slipping because he hadn't turned in several assignments in his English and health classes. When I asked him why, he answered very matter-of-factly, "I didn't think they were due yet. The teachers only told us once." In elementary school where he was reminded many times about when things were due, he had learned to more or less ignore the first few announcements—a bad plan for middle school. On Mondays, each of his teachers would go over the week's upcoming work with their students, who were instructed to write down these assignments.

To ensure that Mike made note of upcoming assignments, projects, and tests, we added the following terms to his contract: he would receive 10 points for bringing this list home on Monday and 10 points for discussing the list and coming up with a reasonable schedule that allowed him to get everything done on time. Each day we referred to this schedule to see if he was keeping pace. He could earn 2 points per day for being up-to-date. He could earn a total of 30 points per week that could be turned in for weekend rewards. Each weekend reward cost 15 points. We also included doing chunks of schoolwork

(15 to 30 minutes depending on the subject), which earned free time. Finishing his schoolwork earned Mike the privilege of staying up 30 minutes later. This contract helped Mike learn to pay attention the first time an assignment was announced, follow a schedule, and turn things in on time. And since he loved staying up later, his contract motivated him to finish his homework. In a later chapter, we'll look at how Mike and I tailored his contract to deal with other areas of concern as they arose.

Brief General Contract

If your teen is self-reliant and usually takes the initiative, a detailed, comprehensive contract may be overkill. You may feel more comfortable with a brief written and signed contract that contains few clauses. Putting your expectations in writing helps make explicit what you want and expect from your teen. Such a contract can serve as validation that things are going well.

In such a general contract, you can briefly describe the safety and school rules you expect your teen to follow. Indicate that if your teen continues to comply with these rules, he will get to keep doing any approved activities he likes. You may use the same approach with family rules. This almost totally hands-off approach is obviously not for every teen but it can work for the older teen who has shown you responsible behavior over a period of time.

In some cases you may not want to use a *written* contract at all, reasoning that your teen understands the rules and follows them, in return for which she is allowed to engage in approved activities. You may not need to monitor her schoolwork by using a contract, but instead allow her to schedule her time and finish her work on her own. However, even if you don't have the rules in writing on a contract, reviewing them occasionally is never a bad idea. If nothing else, such a discussion of rules helps clarify whether you and your teen are on the same page.

Brief General Contract

I, _____ , agree to follow
    safety rules
    school rules
    and family rules

in return for which I will be allowed
    to continue enjoying approved activities
    and to be in charge of my own schedule.

Signed _____ Date _____

I/We, _____ , parent(s) of _____ ,
agree to abide by the terms of this contract.

Signed _____ Date _____

If you're lucky enough to be in the kind of situation that calls for a general contract, congratulations to you and your teen. It's usually a good idea to work together with your teen as you write out your agreement. You're likely to get a few comments about how obvious all this is, as well as questions about what the point is. To me the point is to make certain that you and your teen see eye to eye. Sometimes you'll discover that you don't agree on one of the rules. When this happens, take some time to sort out your different interpretations.

You don't need to revise this kind of general contract very often. If from time to time you have questions about how well your teen is complying, check in with her and discuss your concerns. And, of course, let your words and actions communicate to your teen how much you appreciate her efforts. Of course from time to time you can suggest that your teen deserves something special for acting so responsibly.

Using a Brief General Contract

Let's look at how Fred and Ellen Ward developed a general contract with their 17-year-old daughter, Ashley. Although the Wards were using a comprehensive detailed contract with their 14-year-old son, Drew, to help him follow school and safety rules, they hadn't considered making up a contract for Ashley. Drew took exception to Ashley's exclusion, which he expressed in his usual forthright manner: "How come I have to have a contract with rules when Ashley can do whatever she wants?" Although it seemed to Drew that Ashley didn't have any rules, this was far from true. However, unlike Drew, Ashley was able to follow her rules on her own. Unsatisfied with this explanation, Drew pushed for things to be fair. He wanted Ashley to have a contract too. When Ellen mentioned Drew's concerns to Ashley, she said she didn't mind having a contract. She added that perhaps her contract would show Drew once and for all that she did have rules, that she followed them, and that she didn't get away with everything as Drew thought she did.

Working together, Ellen and Ashley came up with a contract similar to the brief contract you read about above. After a few weeks, Ellen asked Ashley if she'd like something special for being so accountable. Initially Ashley declined the offer, reasoning that she would have been just as accountable without the contract. Her mom replied, "Of course you would have, but I think you deserve some recognition for being responsible." On second thought, Ashley agreed. "OK, how about a shopping trip?" Ellen and Ashley loved to shop together, so this was the perfect reward.

Limited Contract

You may decide that your contract only needs to address one problem area. Such a focused contract can be effective if your teen's primary problem concerns motivation. For example, this kind of contract can work if your teen has been a good student over the years and suddenly quits applying himself in spite of the fact that he is capable of doing his schoolwork. What you need in this situation is a teen who has the skills to correct the problem and a surefire reward that he can only obtain by doing his schoolwork.

Using a Limited Contract

For John Wu, this type of limited contract worked quickly with his 15-year-old son, Charlie, an honor student who was refusing to do his schoolwork and talked only of playing golf. Charlie's belligerence over school and his insistence on golfing were beginning to erode the good relationship he and his father had always shared. Charlie's grades were dropping and all he and his father did was argue about school. John refused to let Charlie

Limited Contract

I, _____ , agree to do the following: _____ for
which I will be rewarded as follows: _____.

Signed _____ Date _____

I/We, _____ , the parent(s) of _____ , agree
to offer the above reward as long as _____ does the following:

_____

Signed _____ Date _____

play golf because he was doing so poorly academically. When Charlie and his dad met with me, we drafted a contract that rewarded Charlie for maintaining at least a B+ average by allowing him to play golf three times a week. How did they do this? John asked Charlie to tell him when his GPA was back up to a B+. At that point John gave Charlie a note for each of his teachers on which they wrote down Charlie's current grade. Charlie willingly showed his father all his quizzes, tests, and papers as evidence that his grades were high enough. To the amazement of all concerned, Charlie's school problems disappeared, his arguing dramatically decreased, and he became a good golfer. Everyone was happy. The contract was able to achieve a rapid turnaround because, although he was only 15, Charlie already had the ability and skills to do well in school. What he needed was renewed motivation. (Again, for a teen who characteristically struggles with school, I recommend a contract that rewards the process of studying, not the GPA.)

Contract Commonalties

Although the scope and format of the contracts you're going to read about are different, they all share some important features. The terms of each contract offers the teen involved a realistic chance of earning rewards right away as well as an impetus for longer-term rewards.

No matter what contract format you decide on, don't fill out the sections dealing with incentives. Although you may want to fill in the number of points earned for following family rules and the number of daily and weekly activities that can be earned for following safety and school rules, I recommend you leave the other sections blank until you and your teen are negotiating. Together you can fill out contract terms such as rewards and point values. If you've decided everything ahead of time and have written it down on the contract, your teen won't feel like she has any input and won't be as invested in

Contract

I, Charlie Wu, agree to do my schoolwork and maintain a B+ average in return for which I get to play golf three times per week.

Signed _____ Date _____

I, John Wu, parent of Charlie Wu, agree to allow Charlie to play golf three times per week as long as he does his schoolwork and maintains a B+ average.

Signed _____ Date _____

To Do

Copy: In Appendix A, you'll find a copy of each contract format, one of which you may want to use as the basis of your format. You can tailor the format in whatever manner you like and delete from or add to any section.

Fill out: Include information you want on your contract format when you begin negotiations with your teen. Keep the section on rewards blank until you and your teen have had a chance to discuss them.

Save: Keep in a safe place. You'll need it soon. You and your teen will work together to fill out this document during contract negotiations.

the contract. She'll feel that your claims that the contract involves interactive negotiation are no more than hollow words.

Making Up Your Contract Format

Using the guidelines you just read about, it's time for you to make up your contract format.

Before you present your contract to your teen, let's take a look at how you can ensure that your contract comes to life and becomes an integral part of your family's daily routine. After all, if your contract is going to work, it needs to be up and running from morning to night. The next chapter provides tips on how to breathe life into your contract.

7

Incorporating Your Contract into Your Family's Routine

Before you talk with your teen about your contract, think through a typical day for ways to incorporate the contract into your daily routine. This will make the transition to using your contract smoother, although some bumps are inevitable.

Your Contract 24/7

Contracts don't work unless your teen follows the rules and *earns* rewards. While this may sound like a simple idea, putting it into practice 24 hours a day, seven days a week, is far from easy. Especially when you're getting started, you may have to work harder to ensure that good behavior happens. And remember, you're likely to be asking your teen to change some ingrained bad habits, so the process can take a long time and may require that you give reminders before the behavior as well as rewards after the behavior.

In general, be as positive and upbeat as you can. Don't look at your contract as an imprisonment but rather as a means of empowering your teen. Don't view your contract as a declaration of war; rather, think of it as a peace treaty. Here are some specific ways you can enhance the effectiveness of your contract as you go through the daily business of living.

- **Start the day on a positive note.** Good vibes in the morning can have a trickle-down effect on the rest of the day. It helps if you get up in plenty of time to get yourself ready as well as to be around as needed by your teens. I've found my resolve to be pleasant in the morning has more than paid off.

  I have never been a morning person and neither have my sons, Mike and Sean. But long ago I realized it was in my best interest to fake it. It was up to me to act pleasant and accommodating because life is so much better when everyone gets up, gets ready, and gets out on time without major hassles. In fact, the whole day seems to go better if the morning isn't a disaster.

  When my sons were in middle school, this meant I knocked on their bedroom doors and, in as nice and pleasant a voice as I could muster at such an early hour, alerted them that wake-up time was coming in 5 to 10 minutes. Sometimes this was enough. If not, I'd return and remind them it was time to get up. As they got older, they set their own alarm clocks and usually got up on their own. And even when they were much too old to need my help, I still got up so I could be around as they ate breakfast and packed their backpacks. Although for a while we used a contract to ensure that good morning behavior was rewarded, it didn't take long until earning points or credits wasn't necessary, as the pleasant interaction was rewarding enough and motivated all of us to get up, get along, and get going.

We've all heard that it's important to send kids off to school with a warm breakfast. (I must confess that I rarely comply with this suggestion.) In my mind, sending my sons off to school after a "warm" morning routine, one that is pleasant and not fraught with conflict, is even more important. Wishing them a good day as they leave for school is lovely. Who knows what trials and tribulations await them at school? Why not send them off with encouragement and support? This doesn't have to be sappy and corny. Be yourself, but be pleasant in your own style. Most teens admit that they feel more prepared to face the day when they've had such a positive sendoff.

- **Make the most of after-school or after-work time.** There are plenty of opportunities during the day for you to connect with your teens, enhance the effectiveness of your contract, and do some bonding as well. For example, when you and your teen intersect for the first time since morning—whether it's after school, late afternoon, or dinnertime, and whether it's at home, in the car, or on the phone—I encourage you to let her know how nice it is to see her and show interest in her day. Avoid cross-examinations and inquisitions. Instead, listen and show interest. Your teen may welcome the chance to blow off steam and talk about her day. Or she may enjoy the opportunity for a little quiet downtime after a hectic day at school. Plan on making this your teen's time, a time when you are available if she wants to talk. Whether you share a silence, a joke, a silly conversation about nothing, whether you decide on what to have for dinner or discuss world peace, by being together and acknowledging each other in positive ways, you're empowering each other and communicating effectively. To repeat an essential point, successful communication does not have to involve heavy, serious issues. In fact, to rebuild and strengthen your relationship with your teen, it's a good idea to start with mundane, conflict-free subjects before doing battle with complicated emotionally charged issues. After this transition time, you and your teen may find it useful to consult your contract/schedules and plan out the remainder of the afternoon and/or evening.

Let's see what happened when single father Leon Carter came to me because he was concerned that he wasn't relating to his 13-year-old son, Jeremy. As Leon described his interactions with Jeremy, it became clear that the moment he got home from work, Leon felt compelled to be sure everything was going OK with his son. Unfortunately, this concern caused Leon to take on the persona of a private investigator who wanted all the facts. No sooner would Leon open the door than the inquisition would begin. Jeremy often became very defensive and clammed up or muttered a quick "yes" or "no" while Leon kept firing away with his questions. How did the math test go? Had Jeremy finished his English paper? Did he score any goals at soccer practice? Did he think he'd be starting as fullback in Saturday's game? Had he called his lab mate about their physical science project? Although I applauded Leon for his concern over his son's progress in school and sports, I suggested he take it more slowly. I recommended he let Jeremy know how nice it was to see him and then ask him generally how he was doing, letting Jeremy have time to answer or not. For the first 15 minutes or so when he was home, I encouraged Leon to keep it light and spontaneous. Let the conversation go wherever it went.

Difficult as this was for Leon, he gave it a try. Initially he felt very uncomfortable because his interaction with his son was not task-oriented. Eventually, however, Leon experienced these casual conversations as productive. Jeremy started opening up and sharing with him. Jeremy confided in me that because his dad was no longer pushing him all the time, he felt much more comfortable talking with him. By spending these unstructured relaxed moments with his son, Leon was enhancing the effectiveness of Jeremy's structured contract and developing a better relationship with his son.

- **Make dinnertime rewarding.** If you eat together, which I strongly recommend, try to make dinner pleasant by not putting anyone on the spot and not insisting that your teen tell you how her day went. She will tell you if and when she's ready and not before. Badgering her to talk almost always backfires and produces a sullen, silent teen. Certainly you can try to initiate conversations, as long as you're prepared for disagreements and debates. Mealtime can be a great time for family discussions on anything and everything. I often used dinnertime to ask about the latest teen styles, not in a judgmental way but in a curious way. Whether it was baggy, oversized pants, skintight miniskirts, or purple hair, we'd all chime in with our opinions. These discussions provided a favorite forum for my older son to champion an individual's right to express himself in whatever manner he wished. The whole family is at a loss to explain the upside of tongue studs.

  Over dinner, you can also bring up how your day went as a way of sharing that you have bad as well as good days. You can admit to making a mistake and explain how you tried to make up for it. You can express disappointment about a frustration, admit that you felt like slugging your boss but realized that such action would not be a good idea and instead held your tongue. These admissions show your teens that you're human, that you have feelings and struggle to express them in socially acceptable ways. Of course you'll also want to share some of the positives of your life—feeling a sense of accomplishment at work, the joy of learning something new, and the satisfaction of doing something well. Hopefully these discussions will set an example for your teen to follow.

For the last several years the Daleys relayed to me how much they had dreaded dinner together because Terry, 15, and Scott, 12, were always at each other's throats. Parents Claire and Jack felt like referees rather than fellow diners. The Daleys were using a contract that included rewards of free time if Terry and Scott could get along after school, at dinner, and in the evening. Because Scott had a bedtime, he used the free time he had earned to stay up 30 minutes later. Terry no longer had a set bedtime, so she used her free time to talk on the phone. In fact, she was saving up for her own phone line.

Receiving incentives for getting along had slowly improved the atmosphere at dinner. One evening during a conversation about how professional athletes seemed to be excluded from receiving punishment for breaking the law, Terry, who was usually outspoken about such injustices, was very quiet. Her mom asked her if she was OK. Terry responded that she was fine, but just didn't feel like talking. In the past Claire or Jack might have grilled Terry about what was really wrong. Instead they accepted her statement and let her alone. However, Scott couldn't resist the opportunity to chime in with, "Terry's saving her voice for the phone." In the past Terry would have blurted out something like, "You dweeb, you don't know anyone who likes you enough to call you. Loser." And an argument would have ensued. But for some reason Scott's comment struck Terry as funny. She smiled and laughed, adding, "Scott, even though you are obnoxious most of the time, sometimes I've got to admit it, you are funny." To the Daleys this was a breakthrough—their kids were able to joke with each other and keep their composure.

- **Get organized after dinner.** The end of dinner is a good time for parents and teens to review the contract and to discuss what's been accomplished and what still needs to be accomplished. If your teen is earning credits, you can go over how many he earned so far. At this point everyone might want to map out what they have planned for the evening. It's a great time for you to model how you're going to try to organize your evening, including tasks you need to do as well as earned breaks you hope to take. Make sure to find out how much homework your teen has and talk about the earned breaks she hopes to take. Communicate that you're available if necessary and that you'd like to check in from time to time to see how things are going. Make these nice check-ins. Always knock. Ask if it's a good time for a progress report. You can add what you'll be doing and reiterate that you're around. Younger teens typically need more monitoring and structuring than older teens.

  In general it's a good idea to be available but not in your teen's face, especially as she gets older. Let your teen know you're ready and willing to listen or offer assistance if and when she wants it. Of course this means that you shouldn't plan an away-from-home activity more than once or twice a week in the evening, especially if you have teens who are in middle school and likely to be home in the evenings. If you work

outside the home and don't see your teen until dinnertime, I strongly suggest that at least one parent be
home every evening.

Afraid of impinging on his 16-year-old daughter,
Claudia's, space, Frank left her alone unless he had
something he had to say to her. However, the result of
this tactic was that he talked to Claudia only when he
had something critical to say or wanted her to do
something; perhaps she'd forgotten to feed the dog and
take him for a walk, or maybe she needed to get to
work on a report that was due the next day. As far as
Claudia was concerned, if her dad wanted to talk to
her, it wasn't good news he'd be sharing. As a result, she
avoided him whenever possible. I recommended that
Frank have a heart-to-heart talk with Claudia and let
her know that he cared about her and was going to try
to change his ways. I suggested he use the kind of contract you've been reading about. The contract would
reward Claudia for doing things like walking the dog
and finishing reports on time. I also advised him to let
Claudia know that he wanted to be more supportive
and that he was there if she wanted to talk with him
anytime. Claudia agreed to the contract, hoping it
would get her dad off her back. She also requested that
she be allowed to give her dad feedback when he was
veering into heavy-criticism territory. Although leery of
this request, Frank went along with it. As it turned out,
Claudia's feedback helped Frank break his habit of criticizing first and asking questions later. Although some
parents might be uncomfortable with a plan in which
teens are allowed to offer feedback, this wasn't the case
with Frank.

- **Ending the day**. At the end of the day is a good time
  to touch base with your teen and say goodnight. You

can use this time to go over the contract and determine credits and/or rewards earned. You may want to have a brief conversation about what your teen hopes to do with his credits. You should also acknowledge your teen's efforts and thank him. Any additional conversation is your teen's call. He may or may not want to talk at this point.

If you miss out on the opportunity to talk with him, you might want to slip a note under the door or tape one to the bathroom mirror, with a general comment on what went well and how good that made you feel. For some teens a note like "Yesterday was great. Let's try for two in a row" is motivating, while for others it's just too corny. You can use E-mail or leave a message on the answering machine about something you really appreciate about your teen. Variety helps, so mix it up a little, be creative, and have fun letting your teen know you care.

Try to follow the time-worn axiom, "Don't go to bed angry." However, if an argument can't be resolved, table it until morning so both parties have time to sleep on it. You might say something like, "It seems like we really don't agree on this right now. Let's call a truce for tonight and try to reach a consensus tomorrow when we're rested." The next morning do not bring the argument up; in most cases it can wait until later in the day. You can let your teen know that you're ready when he is to see if you can come to a compromise. Perhaps he will decide he was being unreasonable and drop the whole thing and/or will be willing to listen to your options. This happened with Ann and Paul Whitman. Their 16-year-old daughter, Jeannie, had announced that she and some of her friends were going to take the train to the city to see a rock concert the following Saturday evening. It was the first time her parents had heard about it, although

Jeannie claimed she had told them repeatedly that as part of her contract she was saving up for the concert as a weekend reward. Neither Ann nor Paul wanted Jeannie to go because they felt it wasn't safe for a group of 16-year-olds to ride the train in the evening. As they explained to her their reasons for forbidding her to take the train, Jeannie exploded, accused them of not trusting her, ran into her room, and slammed the door. Regaining her composure, Ann knocked on Jeannie's door and let her know she was sorry they had argued, that she was firm in her position that Jeannie not take the train, and that she hoped they could reach some kind of compromise. Paul added that he wanted to declare a truce for the remainder of the evening and they could discuss alternate options the next day. Jeannie reluctantly agreed and said goodnight. As it turned out, none of the girls' parents had given them permission to take the train. After talking to several of the parents, Ann and Paul decided to offer to drive the girls to and from the concert. Jeannie and her friends accepted this compromise and enjoyed the concert. Ann and Paul and the other parents were spared a tense evening of worrying about their teens on the train.

Before you fall asleep at night, be sure to pat yourself on the back and congratulate yourself for getting through the day. If it's been a good day, perhaps you weren't driven crazy by your teenager. But even if it was a bad day, look ahead to a better tomorrow. And no matter how the day went, consider taking a reward just for you. Do something easily available that you enjoy. You might want to read, watch television, meditate, work on a favorite project, write a letter, or delve into cyberspace. By rewarding yourself, you'll keep yourself motivated.

Your Contract on the Weekend

- **Talk with your teen about the rewards he's earned.** As the weekend approaches, you and you teen will probably spend time discussing his plans for the weekend. Many families have found that because they're using a contract, arguments about weekend activities decrease somewhat. Your teen has either earned the privilege or he hasn't, so it's easier for you to stand firm. Within the confines of the contract, whether your teen goes somewhere is up to him, not you. When talking about his plans for the weekend, you can briefly review the terms of the contract that pertain to calling in, weekend curfew, safe destination, and acceptable activities.

- **Make time with your teen to do something you both enjoy.** I'd also recommend that you schedule some time for you and your teen to be together on the weekend, especially younger teens. Try to find something that both of you enjoy—something that's not stressful and that won't embarrass your son or daughter. This might involve something as mundane as driving your teen to and from a sports practice or other extracurricular activity and spending time talking in the car. Or you may want to take your daughter out for breakfast or lunch. Although many teens hate shopping with their parents, some don't. A half-day shopping trip can be fun. Just talking at home, enjoying a movie together, or doing a project can bring the two of you together. The important thing is that your teen likes the activity you'll be sharing with him. This one-on-one time can help you and your teen get to know and appreciate each other. I wouldn't talk about problems during this time unless your teen initiates such a request.

- **Clarify and schedule schoolwork or projects that need to be done.** Also, be sure to check in on any schoolwork that needs to be done by Monday morning. In an attempt to encourage your teen to complete his work before the last minute, you may want to provide an extra reward for getting it done by a reasonable time. Be sure to specify this time.

- **Allow time for your teen to relax by himself or with friends.** It's neither necessary nor advisable to fill your teen's weekend with back-to-back activities. He'll benefit from some rest and relaxation. You will too.

I hope these tips will help make your contract an important part of your family's daily life. To make it easier to remember these suggestions, I've summarized them in a list of Contract Quick Tips, which is included on page 117. My clients as well as my own family have found that this list helps take the worry out of what to do next. In fact, many parents display these quick tips and this list in a handy, easy-to-find space.

Once you have a pretty good idea about how your contract will play out, it's time for you to broach the subject with your teen. The next chapter explains the negotiation process. And if it's any consolation, let me repeat that I'm rooting for you.

Contract Quick Tips for Parents

Every Day Throughout the Day:

Adopt a calm, positive outlook.

Give your teen the benefit of the doubt.

Remind as well as reward following the contract.

Follow through with incentives as well as punishments.

Give your teen and yourself credit for trying.

When possible, enjoy a reward just for you.

In the Morning:

Allow enough time for all to get ready.

Pleasantly remind your teen of what she needs to do.

Give her a positive sendoff.

In the Afternoon (If You're Home with Your Teen):

Let him know you're glad to see him.

Show interest about his day but don't push for information.

Spend some time just being together.

Review what your teen has to do and the credits he can earn.

Encourage him to get started.

When enough credits have been earned, provide a reward.

If You Work and Get Home Around Dinnertime:

Have check-in plan with your teen.

When you get home, let your teen know you're glad to see her.

Allow time for sharing the day's experiences in a relaxed manner.

Review the credits she's earned so far.

At Dinnertime:

Eat together if possible; remind the family to get along.

Avoid conflict, personal arguments, and unpleasantness.

Invite your teen to talk; encourage open, interactive discussions.

Share daily ups and downs, give your teen a chance to do the same.

In the Evening:

Review the contract and status to date.

Have each family member map out the evening.

At least one parent should stay home and be available.

Check in with your teen, monitor her progress if needed, and provide rewards.

At the End of the Day:

End the day on a positive note.

Touch base, acknowledge your teen's efforts.

Go over the contract to determine credits earned/hoped for rewards.

If you miss the end-of-day talk, send a note/E-mail and/or check in next morning.

Pat yourself on the back, you've survived another day.

Review your day and look ahead to tomorrow.

On the Weekend:

Decide together on specific activities your teen has earned.

Make time with your teen to do something you both enjoy.

Schedule a time to complete schoolwork.

Allow time for your teen to relax by himself or with friends.

8

Negotiating with Your Teen

You've worked hard, right? You've said at least one nice thing to your teen every day. You've labored over developing a fair, reasonable contract, with good behaviors that are easy to implement and sought-after rewards. You're starting to hope that maybe things can get better. You're ready for that heart-to-heart with your teen, in which you present your behavior contract and your teen thanks you, says, "It's wonderful. You're the greatest parent(s) in the world." . . . Oops! You must have drifted off. Wake up. Get back to reality. Even if you've made up a contract that's destined for the Hall of Fame of Behavior Contracts, you're forgetting something. You still have a teenager you need to persuade to go along with you and give the contract a try.

CREATING A CONDUCIVE ATMOSPHERE

Let's face it, for many parents selling a teen on a behavior contract is far from easy. The way you present your contract to your teen is critical. That's why this entire chapter is devoted to guidelines and tips on how to talk your teen into giving the contract a try.

Be Open-Minded and Flexible

Be forewarned that initially your teen may be reluctant to talk with you. Her hesitancy is hardly surprising given the fact that so often when parents want to talk with their teen it's because the parents have something *critical* to say. As a result, many teens go to great lengths to avoid talking to their parents at all. In your initial contact it's crucial that you make it clear that this is a different kind of talk. And to help you make sure that it really is different, here are some guidelines to follow. Remember, the way you present the idea of a contract can make it or break it, so please spend time on this section before launching into "the big sell."

- **Don't present the contract negatively or as a threat to shape your teen up once and for all.** In my experience, most teens hate it when their parents preach to them about maturity, responsibility, attitude problems, and proper respect. Avoid these terms and others like them. Instead, let your teen know that you're looking forward to this contract, which will spell out the terms of what you want your teen to do as well as rewards he can earn. Share your optimism and ask your teen to keep an open mind.

- **Acknowledge your responsibility as the initiator and a partner in the contract.** It helps if you concede that you know you have to make some changes and emphasize that you really will be working together. In general, as you discuss the contract, I recommend that you talk with your teen the way that you like to be talked to.

Although this recommendation may sound easy in the abstract, we parents of teens know better, much better. Sometimes, before we're even aware of it, we've flown off the handle and find ourselves defensive and off task. What began as a nice peaceful conversation suddenly exploded into a shouting match. To have a chance at talking your teen into participating in your contract, you may need to take special steps to keep the fireworks from going off.

Extend an Invitation

Invite your teen to join you in working together to make things better. Many of my clients have found that a written note, an E-mail, and/or a message on the answering machine is a good way to make initial contact. This allows your teen time to think over your request and decreases the chances of an immediate "forget it" response. After you've issued your invitation, give your teen at least a day or two to respond. Follow up with a simple question: "Did you get my message?" or "When would be a good time to meet?"

I recommend that as part of your invitation you offer to make some changes in your own behavior. Acknowledge that you're not expecting your teen to be the only one to make compromises. Also, using humor can go a long way in this arduous process. Written, signed, and dated notes give an air of importance to the proceedings, but try not to come across as a heavy.

Consider the following types of invitations depending on what works best with your teen.

- **An emotional invitation.** "I've been reading a book about parents and teens that makes me realize I don't tell you often enough how much I care about you and that I sometimes forget to let you know how proud I am of you. How about giving me a chance to tell you in person? When would be a good time? Love, Mom/Dad."

- **A matter-of-fact invitation.** "We would like to enter into contract negotiations as a way to help us all get along better. You'd get some stuff you want in return for going along with us. It would involve two-sided bargaining. How's that sound? No matter how stupid this may sound, I'd like a chance to talk to you about it. Let's talk about it when the time is good for you. Love, Mom/Dad."

- **A short and to-the-point invitation.** "Things stink. I blew it. I'd like to talk about how to make things better. No tricks, I promise. Let me know when it would be a good time. Love, Mom/Dad."

Arrange a Convenient Time to Sit Down and Talk

- **Make this a special time for you and your teen.** There should be no interruptions, or as few as possible. Keep the focus positive and make your meeting private. Younger brothers and sisters are not invited. If you have more than one teen, meet with each one individually. This is his or her time with you. If both parents meet with their teen, it communicates a united front. Be sure to keep from ganging up two on one with your teen—rather, let him know you're both there because you want to make sure you both understand and follow the contract. If your teen has a very strained relationship with one parent, then perhaps the parent who gets along better with her should begin the negotiation process. Although only one parent may be physically present, it's important to acknowledge that the contract stems from a collaboration of both parents. If you're a single parent, try to find a friend with whom you can share your victories and defeats.

- **If the first meeting is a bust, try again.** Many parents who bomb the first time experience success once their teen comes to the realization that a behavior contract is too good a deal to pass up. And, too, you have a lot of ground to cover; be prepared to break your discussion up into several segments, especially if your teen gets belligerent and/or seems overwhelmed.

- **Begin with a simple thank you.** It's always a good idea to start your first meeting with an acknowledgment that you appreciate your teen taking the time to meet with you.

- **Give a general overview of the concept of a contract and the ways in which you hope it will work.** I recommend you refer to your plan simply as a contract that sets forth the rules you want your teen to follow and the rewards she can earn for complying with them. Here is an example of the kinds of things you might want to say:

  "I'd like us to try something new that should have benefits for both of us. Please hear me out and then I'd like to know what you think of the idea. I'd like us to come up with a contract that provides incentives like activities you enjoy and extra spending money in exchange for you doing things I expect and want you to do. Things like getting up in the morning and getting off to school on time, doing your schoolwork, and coming home on time. A book I'm reading suggests some ways to use a contract so that we can get along better and not be at each other's throats so much. I'd like to give it a try. First let me share what I'd like you to do and then we'll talk about what you would expect or like from us for doing these things." .

- **Offer reassurance and encourage giving the contract a try.** If you've tried other programs that didn't work or were abandoned quickly, your teen may be skeptical about what you're doing and whether you'll stick it out. She may also want to know what the catch is. In other words, she'll want a complete explanation of what she is going to have to do and what she is going to have to give up once this program gets going. Again, reassure her that most teenagers like this kind of contract very much because it offers them positive things.

FILLING OUT THE CONTRACT TOGETHER

The following steps should ensure that you and your teen understand the contract. As always, make this part of the negotiation process as interactive as possible.

- **Show your teen the contract format you've chosen.** Briefly point out and describe each section. Then go over each section in more detail.

- **Clarify the rules of the contract.** Let your teen know what rules you expect her to follow. Be sure to be calm and positive. Approach your teen with the expectation that she'll be able to comply. With each rule, in as brief a fashion as possible, work out a definition that makes it clear to both you and your teen what specifically needs to be done. No matter how detailed you are, you'll find that you need to fine-tune your definition of the rules from time to time. Don't belabor the rules or you'll turn your teen off and she'll lose interest in the contract before it even gets started.

You might say something like this: "There are three types of rules I'd like our contract to cover. Since school is a number-one priority, I want to include going to school on time, doing schoolwork on time, and getting passing grades. After school I expect you to check in with me at work and to comply with the after-school activities we've agreed on." (Discuss whichever of these you want to include.)

"Since I worry and want to make sure you stay safe, I want you to come home on time and to call and check in. We need to come up with a specific curfew time for weeknights and weekends, as well as a schedule of when you need to call in. On the weekends I want to be able to feel like I know where you're going and that what you're doing is safe.

"For the family's sake and so I quit bugging you all the time, we need to develop a system that helps all of us get up in the morning and ready for the day. We also need a plan that encourages all of us to get along better. And perhaps we could come up with a workable schedule of chores that need to get done."

- **Suggest using reminders to help your teen follow the rules.** Because changing any behavior, especially long-standing bad habits, is never easy, your teen may benefit from reminders about the rules of the contract. Ask your teen if he'd like you to remind him about the provisions of his contract as a way of making it easier for everyone to remember. Mention that you'll try to do this in a nonirritating way and that you won't embarrass him in front of siblings or friends.

For example, you might say, "Would you like me to remind you for a while as you're getting used to this change? What would be a good way for me to do this? Some families come up with a code word." My older son always voted for a reminder because he found them helpful; my younger son preferred to go it on his own and was able to remind himself. If your teen doesn't want reminders but has trouble remembering the terms of the contract, you can ask him again. He may change his mind.

Review and Revise the Rewards as Needed

- **Clue your teen in on the rewards and activities you thought of.** You may want to do this by referring to your reward checklist and letting your teen see the rewards you came up with. This sample of rewards gives your teen a general idea of the kinds of activities and purchases you consider appropriate.

- **Ask for your teen's input concerning incentives.** Don't be surprised if your teen comes up with some acceptable rewards you hadn't thought of as well as some outrageous requests. Have your teen jot the acceptable ones down on the reward checklist.

- **Clarify that both of you must agree on a reward before it can be included in the contract.** Your teen may want more freedom or money than you're willing to give her. With any activity she suggests, be sure she knows that before the final OK can be given you'll need to know where she's going, with whom, and how she's getting there. Hold your ground when your teen wants too much. If possible, suggest an alternative you can live with. Listen to her ideas, but be firm on your limits. Explain why you can't approve a specific activity. For example, you may feel the location is too dangerous, that supervision will be inadequate, and/or that she's not ready for activity such as one-on-one dating or driving places with friends.

- **Have your teen jot down any additional approved rewards on the reward checklist.** Once your teen has included her rewards, your list is complete. You'll use this list on a weekly basis to decide on rewards your teen wants to earn. Certainly the list can be revised as needed.

Explain Your Reward System

- **With your teen, go over the kinds of daily and weekly rewards your teen can earn by following a particular rule or set of rules.** Have her choose some rewards for the coming week and write them on the contract. Be certain she's aware of the number of weekday and weekend activities she can earn. Of course she can change her mind about any of the specific activities she lists on the contract as long as you approve her new choices.

- **Review how the point system will work.** Let your teen know how many points he can earn for following each family rule. Specify the value of a point in terms of credits or money. Talk about how many credits are needed to enjoy a certain activity or purchase.

- **Solicit your teen's input and try to be flexible.** If you're unsure about his proposed plan, give yourself some time to think about it. For example, if your teen feels that the price of an activity or purchase is too high, hear him out. You don't want to make the price in credits so high that he isn't motivated.

Keeping Track of Rules Followed and Rewards Earned

Decide how to indicate that rules have been followed. For example, if you're using a comprehensive format, you may be recording compliance with each rule; however, if you're using a briefer contract format you may indicate compliance with each category of rules. You should also review the process for logging the points your teen earns. It's good to write everything down. Keeping track of credits earned and spent reduces misunderstandings and disagreements about where your teen stands.

Presenting Your Discipline Plan

Before you end your discussion of the contract, it's important to talk about the role of discipline. Most teens do not want to hear about what will happen when they goof up, so introduce this area with as much diplomacy as possible. Keep your discussion straightforward and to the point. Do not use a threatening tone. For example, in your calmest manner, you might say something like, "So far we've talked about positive incentives for following the rules. Maybe you're wondering what would happen if you really goofed up by, for instance, coming home an hour or more late, lying about where you're going, or getting an unsatisfactory interim grade. While I certainly don't expect any of these things to happen, if for some reason they do, there will be more serious consequences than just losing credits. Depending on the severity of the infraction, you could be grounded for a period of time. Although I'm confident that you'll make sure to follow the rules, I feel it's only fair to let you know that major slip-ups will be punished accordingly." This serves notice to your teen and lets her know that you feel she's capable of following through, but if she proves you wrong, you will respond with a punishment that fits the crime. Be sure to include discussion of possible grounding for rule infractions. If you leave it out, your teen may erroneously believe that the only consequence for major transgressions would be the loss of a few credits.

When discussing your discipline plan with your teen, give him some specific examples of what you plan to do when he misbehaves. For example, you could let him know that a minor slip-up such as coming home five minutes late will receive a one-time warning. If the offense occurs again, you will make his curfew earlier. Inform him that you'll be ignoring whining, begging, and pleading as well as any arguments concerning the fairness of the contract. Make it clear that if he breaks a rule, he'll lose the points he would have earned. If he violates the rule several times or seriously, a likely consequence will be an earlier curfew or grounding.

Wrapping Up Your Negotiations

- **Have all parties involved sign and date the contract.** This gives the document an air of formality and importance.

- **Give each family member involved a copy of the contract.** Then they can refer to it as a reminder of the agreement you have made.

- **Ask if your teen wants her contract kept private.** Reassure her that you won't share it with anyone unless and until you have her permission. Your daughter may tell a good friend about the contract who in turn will tell her parents. In such cases, the parent may contact you to find out more. Before sharing with anyone, I recommend you run this idea by your teen and get her approval.

- **Explain that contract negotiation is a weekly event.** Let your teen know that the two of you will be reviewing it weekly to check out how well it's working. Suggest that you touch base once or twice daily to determine what's been earned in both daily and weekly rewards. And let your teen know that you plan to meet sometime at the end of the week to finalize earned weekend activities.

- **Together decide when to start the contract.** Sunday evening or Monday morning are popular times to activate your contract. Most teens are ready to begin because of the incentives offered. However, if your teen wants some time to think it over, that's OK too. As a reminder, until the contract goes into effect, your teen can't earn incentives. Don't allow your teen to "sort of go along" with the contract without fully agreeing to it; it's much harder to gauge if and when to provide rewards with such an iffy commitment.

- **Thank your teen for giving the contract a try.** At the end of your meeting, thank your teen for going along with a contract, and again express your enthusiasm. Once you've ironed out your contract with your teen, it's important to acknowledge how pleased you are that the two of you worked together and that you feel she deserves some kind of reward for her efforts. For example, you might offer some friendly words such as, "I think we're on the right track. Thanks for taking the time to meet with me and negotiate your contract. I think your efforts merit a reward." At this point you can offer rewards you're willing to give either immediately or in the future. For example, you might suggest that your teen invite a friend over or spend some extra time on the phone during the evening. If you have a younger teen you can thank him for participating in the negotiation by allowing him to stay up later. If an immediate reward is not feasible, consider giving your teen some credits that can be used later, perhaps on the weekend to buy a reward. I suggest you specify the reward rather than asking your teen to pick one. Since she is new at this, she might very well choose something you consider too extravagant. However, if, after hearing your suggestion, she suggests an alternative reward that meets with your approval, by all means let her have it.

Recognizing your teen's participation is vital because it shows her you are serious about the contract and providing her with incentives for appropriate behavior; in this case, the appropriate behavior was talking with you and hammering out the contract. Even if your interchange was a little rocky, if you were able to agree upon terms, reward your teen. And while you're at it, why not reward yourself as well? You've earned it.

Negotiation Guidelines in Action

Let's look in on several of my clients during phases of their negotiations to give you an idea of how different approaches to negotiation worked.

Emma Wilson was a 13-year-old seventh grader who couldn't seem to follow a workable morning schedule. Her mother and father had full-time jobs and thus had to get themselves ready as well as monitor Emma's every move in hopes she'd get ready on time. Their morning routine had become exasperating and exhausting. The Wilsons felt the time had come for a contract.

Emma got along better with her dad, Gary, than with her mom, Natalie, so Gary assumed the role of negotiator. After talking in general about the contract, Gary introduced the subject of Emma's failure to get ready to leave for school on time.

"Emma, you know how in the mornings we're all rushed trying to get ready to leave? And how we get on your case sometimes when you're running late? I'd like us to come up with a plan that helps you get ready more on your own in the morning. How does that sound?"

Emma seemed lukewarm on the idea; she shrugged, "Well, I'm not late *that* often. OK. What kind of plan are you talking about?"

Wisely, Gary did not argue with Emma about how frequently she wasn't ready to go on time. Instead, he focused on the plan by asking, "What time do you think all of us need to be ready to leave to make sure you get to school on time?"

Emma and Gary agreed on 7:30 A.M. Gary suggested they talk about what Emma needed to do in the morning and whether there was anything that took a long time. Emma shared that she could never decide what to wear and sometimes it took forever to come up with the perfect outfit. Gary suggested that she might try getting up earlier or planning the night before what she would wear and laying the clothes out before she went to bed. Emma was not enthusiastic about getting up earlier but thought maybe choosing her outfit the prior evening might work. If she had questions about what to wear she could call her best friend Carol and talk it over.

Gary asked Emma if she'd like getting an incentive for planning ahead and being ready on time. He suggested credits that could be used for a monthly clothes-shopping trip. Emma thought that sounded great.

This system worked well for the Wilsons. Every evening Emma enjoyed leisurely picking out the clothes she planned to wear and looked forward to her monthly shopping trip. Natalie and Gary no longer had to nag and coax Emma to get ready. Everyone found the morning routine so much more pleasant that they no longer dreaded it and enjoyed the ride to school in the car together. Did the Wilsons really need an incentive system? Maybe not; however, the incentive most likely accelerated Emma's behavior change as it motivated her to get up and get going.

Negotiating the Hard Sell

Sometimes a teen can be a hard sell, as the Kim family discovered. Their 15-year-old daughter, Allison, was very headstrong, dramatic, and opinionated. She and her parents were at odds concerning almost everything. When the parents, Cordelia and Warren, presented the idea of a contract, Allison was, not surprisingly, her usual belligerent self. During their contract negotiations, Allison suggested an absurdly late curfew and a hefty expense account. Unfortunately, several of her friends had very nonattentive, indulgent parents; these kids got to do and buy pretty much whatever they wanted. Allison frequently used these friends as examples of the privileges she should be allowed. Her parents let Allison rant that other kids didn't have to follow stupid babyish rules like the ones in the contract. Cordelia and Warren just listened and didn't interrupt as Allison railed that they didn't own her. In spite of her protests, her parents held firm and repeated, "When you're ready to talk about the contract, let us know. There will be a contract and until we sit down and talk about it, consider yourself grounded every weeknight and weekend night." Allison blurted out, "See if I care. You never let me go anywhere," as she stormed out of the room.

When I met again with the Kims they were understandably concerned that a contract might not work out with Allison. I asked them to hang in there because there still might be hope.

I've found that in cases where teens can't talk to their parents without cannons going off, putting things in writing can be helpful. Together Cordelia, Warren, and I drafted a letter to Allison that explained the purpose and nature of the contract they had in mind. In the letter, we included an invitation for Allison to come and talk with me so that I could hear her side of the story. Allison did pay me a visit. She told me that because her parents were very strict and always coming down with punishments for even the smallest things she did wrong, she had expected a complicated formula that outlined accelerating groundings for rule infractions. Instead, she discovered that she could earn incentives for following the rules. She wanted to know if her understanding of the contract was correct. She also wanted to make sure the contract was legit and not a setup. I assured her that her interpretation of the contract was accurate and that it was for real. Convinced her parents wanted to turn over a new leaf, Allison agreed to meet with them.

The Kims had already realized that they had gotten into the habit of almost never noticing Allison's strong points. One of the reasons they had wanted to negotiate a contract with their daughter was that it would help them pay attention and reward the good things Allison did. The family had some heated discussions about rewards and acceptable activities, but eventually they were able to come to terms over school and safety rules, including curfew time, that were acceptable to everyone. Allison was especially pleased with two of her incentives. If she got home by curfew for two weeks, she could attend a rock concert. The only restriction was that she allow one of her parents to drive her and friends to and from the concert. As an added reward, if Allison complied with school and safety rules for four weeks, she would earn an extended curfew of 30 minutes on one weekend night. Crossing their fingers, the Kims launched Allison's contract. And they were pleasantly surprised. Although Allison still fought for what she wanted, her demands

To Do

When you feel ready, using the guidelines you read about as well as the experience of the families discussed, begin negotiations with your teen and fill out his/her contract. Good luck.

became more realistic. Unlike during her precontract days, she was willing to listen to her parents' views.

As you read about their negotiations with Allison, you may have wondered why the Kims allowed Allison to talk to them as she did. You may feel that they gave her too much power and let her show too much disrespect. The Kims had a goal, and they stuck to it. They wanted to get a contract up and running, and if that meant temporarily ignoring some ranting and raving, they were willing to do it. Certainly if Allison had continued this type of surly behavior they would have addressed it in the contract under the category of getting along with family members. As it turned out, when Allison's anger began subsiding because she was being allowed privileges and not being constantly grounded, her behavior toward her parents improved markedly. If she did start to yell or whine, her mother and father found that a calm request that everyone try to get along was enough to get Allison back on a more positive track.

Pleasant dreams. Before you know it, tomorrow, day one of the contract will be upon you. Here's to a new beginning.

The next part helps you welcome this fresh start by showing you how to use your contract week by week to increase your teen's good behavior.

PART IV

YOUR CONTRACT
IN ACTION

9

Encouraging Good Behavior

This chapter will begin by covering tips to help you navigate the unpredictable and most likely wildly fluctuating waters of your first month using your contract. No matter how great your contract is and how much enthusiasm your family has, the first several weeks can be especially challenging for all concerned as everyone, yourself included, is getting used to a new system.

GETTING YOUR CONTRACT UP AND RUNNING

As you begin your first week and those thereafter, here are some tips to help you through each day.

- **Begin the day with a positive outlook.** It helps if you can start each day in a positive frame of mind. Recognize that everyone is just getting started and that it will take some time to learn the ins and outs of living with a contract.

Remind yourself that both you and your teen will make mistakes, but if all of you can hang in there, you'll get the gist of contract living. Things *will* get better.

- **Refer to your list of Contract Quick Tips.** These will help you remember what you need to do. If you haven't already done so, please refer to Appendix A and make a copy. Feel free to jot down any additional reminders that make your job as contract manager easier. Check in with these tips throughout the day.

- **Go over the terms of the contract with your teen.** As you go through the first week, it's a good idea to spend some extra time making certain that your teen is clear about the terms of the contract. The better she understands it, the better her chances are of complying with it. Make a point to go over the terms of your contract with your teen on a daily basis at a convenient time, perhaps in the afternoon or early evening. Supply her with a gentle reminder if she seems to need one, whether it's about doing her schoolwork, limiting phone time, or calling to check in after school.

- **Touch base to check on progress.** You should also make an effort to check in with your teen for updates about his progress and the credits he's earned. Acknowledge his efforts with a thank you. Younger teens generally require more frequent checking in than do older teens.

- **Discuss rewards.** Talking with your teen about how she wants to spend her credits either during the week or on the weekend is a good way to keep her interested in her contract because it gives her something positive to look forward to.

- **Don't give unearned rewards.** Don't provide incentives for good intentions or promises. Enforce the terms of the contract. Don't make allowances "just this once." If you do, you'll be teaching your teen that his contract isn't for real. If your teen violates the contract, follow through with a punishment that fits the crime. Don't let him talk you out of it. Don't excuse him for coming home late, not doing his schoolwork, or fighting with his brother—just because he's getting used to the contract or he forgot doesn't excuse the behavior. Letting him off the hook will interfere with his learning to comply with the contract. He won't take you or the contract seriously.

- **Don't take away rewards that have been earned.** Even if you're totally furious with your teen, don't strip her of the credits or privileges she's already earned. Taking away earned credits will weaken your contract. Your teen will not trust you; she'll feel you have violated the contract. For example, if your daughter has been doing well earning credits for following family rules but then suddenly has an awful day during which she seems to be working hard to infuriate you, don't revoke her credits just because you're angry with her. If emotions are running high and no one is able to speak without war breaking out, postpone her opportunity to spend her credits until things have settled down.

- **Continue your talk times.** Don't fill them up with discussion of the contract. Instead, leave enough time to share the events of the day, the ups and the downs, or a silly joke. You and your teen need nonfocused, non-business time together. Such unstructured time will be a welcome change from the structure of the contract.

In addition, it will actually enhance the effectiveness of your contract.

- **Keep in contact with your buddy.** Make an effort to talk out problems, concerns, or questions with your spouse or a friend. It's important that you have someone to hash things out with. Even if you argue over what's the best thing to do, it's good to have a second opinion on what is happening. It also can help put things in perspective. You may feel like you're getting nowhere until your buddy points out that some progress has indeed taken place.

- **Don't forget to reward yourself.** Of course, your teen's improvement is gratifying and rewarding when it happens, but don't forget to reward yourself for your time and effort—on a daily basis if possible. Having something to look forward to will help you get through the difficult days and shore up your motivation to continue. So do it. Reward yourself.

Offering an Extra Reward

Sometimes you may feel your teen deserves an extra reward. Offering a surprise reward from time to time can boost everyone's spirits. You can use an added incentive to acknowledge a particularly good week and/or to show appreciation for your teen's efforts.

Let's see how the Talbots put this idea into action with their 15-year-old daughter, Sarah. Pleased with her efforts at cleaning her room, the Talbots taped the following note on Sarah's bedroom door: "The management thanks you for your valiant efforts in room maintenance and would like to acknowledge this endeavor appropriately. Any ideas? When pondering, please keep the family motto in mind—'Think small.' Love, Mom and Dad."

Laughing as she read the note, Sarah kidded her parents, "No matter how many notes you send me I'll never be a neatnik." Her mom broke into a smile as she responded, "Sarah, I've known you for over 15 years, and trust me, there's no way your dad or I could turn you into a neatnik no matter what we did. But we did want to acknowledge your efforts. Can you think of an extra reward you'd like?" After thinking for a few minutes, Sarah decided on a "husband"—one of those pillows that's like the top of an armchair. And although she wouldn't admit it to her parents just yet, Sarah kind of liked her room being less messy. She didn't have to keep throwing piles of clothes and stuff from place to place as she looked for things or tried to sit down.

If your teen has had a trying week at school, you may want to show your appreciation and offer to contribute to a weekend reward. My clients, the Grays, found sending E-mails such as the following were a good way to acknowledge their 17-year-old son's academic efforts: "Reese, What a week! Three tests and a report in five days. Yikes! Hopefully you have plans to kick back and take it easy this weekend. You've earned it. We'd like to help out by making a contribution. Let us know. A trip to Las Vegas is not an option and other limitations apply. Guess who?" Corny, yes, but it got their point across.

Exhausted from his week, Reese appreciated his parents' acknowledgment. Like most teens he rather enjoyed positive feedback for his efforts. When he read the note he was too tired even to imagine doing anything other than sleeping. However, by Saturday morning he was revitalized and was looking forward to the football game and school dance. As an extra reward, he asked if he could get a new sweatshirt for the festivities. His parents agreed, so he took the car and bought what he considered to be a totally awesome shirt.

Using Your Contract on the Weekend

Ideally, the weekend is a time to celebrate the victories of the week. It's a time to acknowledge good behavior by providing weekend activities as rewards. Hopefully your teen will have earned enough credits during his first week with the contract to do something on the weekend.

- **Meet to talk with your teen about weekend plans.** Talk with your teen throughout the week about his progress toward earning weekend rewards. It's also a good idea to schedule a meeting at a convenient time near the end of the week to talk more specifically about your teen's weekend plans. Some families meet as early as Thursday night; others wait until Friday afternoon or evening or Saturday morning.

   This meeting can serve a number of functions. Certainly one of the main ones is to let your teen know how much you appreciate his efforts at complying with the contract. As always, be positive and upbeat that he did so well.

- **Decide together on specific activities your teen has earned.** Give your teen the chance to decide on how she's going to spend her earned credits and/or to choose the weekend activities in which she wants to participate. Get as many specific details as you can about the activities your teen plans to participate in. Find out where she plans to go and what she plans to do. If she needs transportation and you can provide it, I recommend you do so and/or share this task with another trusted parent. As noted before, plans may change by the minute. Expect this and roll with it as best you can. No matter how many different scenarios you've been exposed to, your teen needs to settle on one concrete plan before she leaves the house. Double-check her plans before she takes off and make sure you're in agreement about curfew time.

- **Schedule a time to complete schoolwork.** To avoid ruining a wonderful weekend with an unpleasant Sunday night spent arguing about your teen's unfinished schoolwork, I recommend that you and your teen map out a schedule—one that allows him to enjoy his rewards but also gives him enough time to complete any necessary school-related tasks.

- **Make time with your teen to do something you both enjoy.** This time should be fun and shouldn't depend on your teen's performance on the contract. Don't even talk about the contract. No matter how well or how poorly your teen did during the week, try to spend some pleasant, positive time with her on the weekend.

- **Allow time for your teen to relax by himself or with friends.** Don't encourage your teen to plan out every minute of his weekend with back-to-back activities. Encourage downtime. Unstructured time can be rejuvenating for your teen (and for you as well).

USING YOUR CONTRACT FROM WEEK TO WEEK

Keep abreast of your teen's progress from week to week. To ensure this, set up a weekly routine to review, renegotiate, and restart your teen's contract. The following guidelines should help you make this weekly task a consistent and productive interchange with your teen.

- **Evaluate your teen's progress.** At the end of each week, take a few minutes to review the contract and how well your teen did. Don't expect miracles or a perfect performance. Hopefully, over time your teen will earn more points and get to enjoy more activities.

If your teen was able to earn an average of three or more points per day during the past week, stick with your contract for the upcoming week. If your teen averaged fewer than three points per day, consider adding a category/rule with which she'll be likely to comply. By making this addition, you're increasing the odds that your teen will earn at least a few points and experience a reward for her good behavior. For your teen's contract to work in the long run she needs to experience the relationship between her good behaviors and good consequences, not just between her problem behaviors and negative consequences. If she experiences only the negative links she may lose motivation and quit trying altogether.

Don't expect to like your teen any better after the first few weeks, nor should you assume that your teen will suddenly find you wonderful. Changes in feelings and attitude can take a long time. Right now your concern is changes in your teen's behavior. And you can measure objectively these changes by looking at points earned and activities enjoyed.

- **Make a copy of your contract format.** Each week have a fresh copy of the contract format you and your teen will be filling out.

- **Set up a meeting time.** Schedule a specific time to meet with your teen and go over her contract for the coming week. A Sunday afternoon or evening meeting works well for many families. Try to come up with a regular, consistent time each week.

- **Sit down with your teen.** Begin your meeting with a general statement that expresses your enthusiasm and appreciation for your teen's efforts. Although you may feel things are going better, keep this opinion to yourself. Your teen will let you know if and when he thinks things are better. Avoid comments such as, "I knew it would work. I knew you'd like it. Aren't things better?" Don't expect your teen to validate or echo your positive assessment.

- **Review the contract with your teen, and concentrate on what went right.** As noted earlier, if your teen has averaged less than three points per day, you should add a rule with which she has a high likelihood of complying. Otherwise keep the contract the same. Even if your teen did fabulously, don't make it harder, not yet.

    If your teen has been very compliant, she may ask that you extend her privileges, perhaps set a later curfew. It's too soon to do this. Although her requests may be options you'll consider in the future, for now curfew and other privileges should remain the same. However, it's OK for your teen to suggest different rewards as long as they're comparable with the rewards she earned the first week.

    If your teen slipped up and you invoked an earlier curfew or a weekend grounding, try talking calmly and specifically about what your teen did that resulted in this consequence. Express your hope and optimism that she'll be able to follow the rules during the coming week and so avoid being grounded and enjoy a regular curfew.

- **Go over how the contract will work for the next week.** Talk about the different activities or rewards your teen may want. If your teen is not sure of what rewards he wants to earn, that's fine. He has all week to make up his mind, providing of course that you agree on his decisions.

- **Sign and date the contract.** Both of you should sign and date the contract. This can serve as an official restart.

This general outline should serve you well, at least for the first four weeks—and hopefully beyond.

Going Beyond the First Month

- **Don't rush into any revisions of your rules.** Although some families are in a hurry to revise their contracts after the first month, I don't recommend it. If during the first month your teen showed gradual improvement, stick with what you've got. Don't feel you have

To Do

Evaluate: Look over your teen's contract. Make a note of the points he earned and the activities he's enjoyed.

Copy: Make a fresh copy of the contract format you're using.

Meet with your teen: Specify a time to sit down together and go over the contract.

Review: Go over his progress. Highlight his positive accomplishments.

Preview: Talk about the upcoming week. Decide on any changes, and discuss rewards your teen wants to earn.

Fill out: With your teen, fill out the contract and sign it. Make sure each of you retains a copy of the contract.

Get started: Begin the contract for the next week.

to make any major changes in your teen's contract. She's still getting used to following the rules, and there's no point in making things harder. Appreciate your success, but don't tempt fate by increasing the stakes. Most teens have enough stress at school as schoolwork gets harder and harder. They don't need their parents joining this bandwagon at home.

Let's check in again with the Jeffersons and their son, Joe, who began his contract at age 13. The contract initially focused on helping him adjust to his new, more difficult middle school schedule. Because Joe loved baseball, his rewards tended to revolve around playing baseball and buying sports equipment. Although the Jeffersons were tempted to move on to other areas, they found that if they eased up concerning Joe's schoolwork, his performance suffered. Joe's contract stayed almost the same for the three years he was in middle school. As a reward for studying and finishing his schoolwork, he was allowed to go out for baseball, attend practices, and play in the twice-weekly games. As long as Joe's contract was working, there wasn't any reason to change it.

- **You may want to extend rewards.** If your teen has faithfully followed the rules and arrived home on time for a month, you can consider extending her curfew by 30 minutes. Such action on your part is a message that you trust her to do the right thing. Most teens consider a later curfew a sign of respect and a nod to their maturity. So if your teen has earned it, talk to her about making curfew later. You may also want to double-check other privileges your teen has been earning and consider expanding these. Again, go slowly.

- **Otherwise keep your contract the same.** Why mess with success? If your teen is doing a good job at following your contract and if your relationship is beginning to show signs of improvement, don't rock the boat.

- **Celebrate your victories.** This section is included to alert you to the importance of formally acknowledging the family's accomplishments. I've worked with far too many families who didn't think they really deserved to celebrate. Things could always be better. Even though you may have many more goals ahead, you and your family deserve a pat on the back for your efforts. If nothing else, your time, effort, and patience deserve some official recognition. And what about your teens? They've hung in there and made a go of it. They should be in line for some congratulations as well. So from time to time, make an effort to give the whole family credit for following along with the contract. Such teamwork deserves a "hip, hip, hooray"—or the teenage equivalent, whatever that is in your family.

USING YOUR CONTRACT OVER TIME

- **Meeting challenges.** As you use your contract from month to month and year to year, you'll find that you're likely to revise your teen's contract to incorporate the new challenges he faces. Over the years your contract can help your teen adjust to middle school and high school. It can accommodate your teen as he moves from supervised group activities to dating. It can follow your teen as he gets transported by you, practices driving, and then drives himself. It can help your teen organize his life and his time.

- **Phasing out hands-on elements of the contract.** As your teen gets older, your contract may not need to be as formal. This happens when your teen is comfortable with what you want and is complying; has learned and experienced how self-rewarding mastering academic skills and taking responsibility for herself can be; and uses good judgment about out-of-home activities. It happens when he tries to solve problems on his own but comes to you for advice when needed. You and your teen don't agree on everything, but for the most part you agree on the important stuff and can talk through most of your disagreements. You respect one another. You look out for each other. The contract functions at a more informal level. There's no longer any need to pair up behaviors with rewards. The relationship is ingrained in parents and teen alike.

Let's see how, over the years, the Grants used their contract with their daughter, Erika.

The Grants began using a contract with Erika when she was 12. Initially they focused on her schoolwork and her behavior around the house, using a contract to help her develop responsibility in these areas. Earning incentives had definitely helped Erika take responsibility for completing her homework, writing reports, and studying for tests.

Her contract had also helped Erika take responsibility for doing her own laundry and putting it away. Although she balked at keeping her room orderly, she did make sure to remove trash and gather up the dirty laundry when it was laundry time. Erika pointed out that she knew where everything was and that rooms have doors for a good reason. Her parents decided that any additional efforts on their part to improve room maintenance would be a losing battle to wage. One of Erika's favorite ways of spending the money she earned was to save up for creative decorations for her room. She used her earned credits to transform her room and express herself. Over the years she went through a black-light-and-glowing-stars phase, a young-movie-star-poster stage, and finally a European Impressionist period.

By the time Erika turned 15, she had become a good student. She and her parents felt she was ready to move on to maintaining an agreed-upon grade point average. Erika and her parents decided on a B average. Erika was sure she could do better, but her parents felt that requiring a higher average might put too much stress on her. As long as Erika's average was a B, she could continue to participate in the extracurricular activities she loved—soccer, drama, and journalism club.

In addition, when Erika turned 15, much of her focus was on the fact that she would be able to drive the following year. As an incentive in her contract, she asked for driving lessons, which her parents were happy to include. At this point the focus of Erika's contract shifted to behaving responsibly away from home. Erika had proven to her parents that she was responsible and could follow through and comply with rules. The Grants were willing to listen carefully to her requests for more freedom. At 15, Erika was allowed to go places with groups of girls and boys provided that the activity was safe and/or there was adult supervision. As she grew older she was allowed to go out with a date in a group. As a high school junior she was allowed to date as long as the boys were no more than a year older than she was. When she got her driver's license, she and her parents came up with a contract covering driving, which specified terms of responsible driving, such as keeping the speed limit, driving in a certain radius, wearing a seat belt, and following the rules of the road. Erika got to use the car two to three times per week—as long as she followed the rules of her contract.

The Grants used their contract with Erika to encourage her to assume responsibility, first at home and at school and then away from home when driving and with friends. Although the contract didn't guarantee peace at all times, Erika and her parents had many fewer conflicts than most families. As an added benefit, because they were on reasonably good terms, Erika felt much more comfortable talking to her parents about issues that bothered her. These talks allowed the Grants to share their values and perspectives with Erika in a nonjudgmental and positive way.

By the time she was 16, Erika had internalized the terms of her contract. She followed the rules without any reminding. She didn't need the external structure of a written contract. She carried the rules in her head. It wasn't necessary to jot down rewards each week. She let her parents know ahead of time where she was going and what she was doing. If her parents were unsure they agreed on her plans, the three of them sat down and talked about the situation in detail. They were almost always able to resolve their disagreements. When Erika's parents weren't comfortable with her plans, they explained exactly why. Since Erika respected her parents, she went along with their wishes even if she didn't agree with their point of view. It's important to note that her parents rarely opposed her proposed activities.

When I asked Erika and her parents if they thought they'd be getting along as well as they were if they'd never used a contract, they were quick to respond. "I doubt it," they chimed in unison. Playing devil's advocate, I replied, "But you can't be sure. Maybe you would have done fine without a contract." "Why would we take that chance?" Erika's mom wanted to know. "The contract helped all of us," her dad added. Erika continued, "At first I thought a contract was a really dumb idea and that Mom and Dad would be watching my every move and never let me do anything. But as it turned out I got to do more than most of my friends who weren't on contracts and who kept getting grounded all the time for even the littlest thing. I think my parents should keep using it with my younger sister Melanie no matter what she says." Although most teens are unlikely to speak so highly of their contracts, over time, they recognize that the positive effects of the contract significantly outweigh the negative effects.

It's not uncommon for teens to experience difficulty following their contract from time to time. The next chapter outlines some steps you can take to help your teen stay on track.

10

Handling Contract Problems and Violations

No matter how fantastic a job you're doing, there *will* be problems and surprises along the way. This first part of this chapter deals with problems your teen or you may have following the contract. The latter portion outlines a step-by-step process for you to use when handling contract violations.

DEALING WITH COMMON CONTRACT PROBLEMS

- **Expect your teen to complain about the contract.** Try your best to ignore this whining. Although at the time of negotiation your teen may have felt the rules were fair and easy to follow, she may change her mind when she's actually expected to comply with them. She may be unpleasantly surprised when you follow through with terms of the contract. If she got to do pretty much whatever she wanted before the contract went into effect, she's unlikely to be pleased by her new rules. Be prepared for statements such as, "How can you be so mean? Jan is counting on me to come over and listen to her new CD. You always let me go before. It's not fair." If your daughter hasn't earned the privilege of visiting a friend, she can't go—not even just this once.

- **Slip-ups are commonplace.** Your contract is probably asking your teen to break bad habits that have been around for a while, so don't be surprised if he reverts to his old habits. He may simply forget the new rules and act as though they're not in effect. For minor infractions, such as not calling in on time or being five minutes late, a warning may be sufficient—especially for first-time occurrences. If these minor infractions continue, you should consider a consequence that is more serious such as making curfew earlier. Whatever you do, try to invoke gradually more severe penalties instead of coming down with something drastic at the first minor slip-up.

- **Don't be surprised if your teen tests the limits.** Your son may intentionally test the limits of his contract to see if you'll follow through. He may forget to call in as promised. He may lose track of time and come home 30 minutes late just to see what will happen. No matter how great your teen's excuse, follow through with the consequences your contract specifies. In addition to losing credits, he may get an earlier curfew or a grounding if he repeatedly or seriously tests the limits.

  For example, I recommend you follow the dictates of your contract; if your son comes home an hour after curfew, don't lecture him on his immaturity and disrespect. Instead calmly state that he has broken the rules of the contract and therefore will be grounded the following night. If he accuses you of being a cruel monster and says he hates you, don't try to make him understand your position. Don't ask for a heartfelt apology you'll never get; leave the room with your buttons safely *not* pushed. In the next chapter we'll look at what to do about repeated offenses that trouble you.

- **Don't forget—you make mistakes too.** Your teen may not be the only one who goofs up; you may as well. If and when you do, I suggest that you apologize and promise to get back on track. Since old habits are hard to break, parents often find themselves falling into negative patterns. This happened to Elena Rosati, who was using a contract with her 15-year-old daughter, Janie.

  As part of the contract, Janie and her mother were focusing on getting along better. Before they began to use the contract it seemed like they spent most of their time together criticizing one another and trading zingers. Although some progress had been made, things were far from perfect, as Janie made sure to let me know.

  Janie was fuming when I saw her. "I told you my mom couldn't follow this stupid contract," she said. "No sooner had our basketball team lost in double overtime than mom ran down on the floor and started ragging on me about how I let the team down, and to make things worse, she did this in front of the team and my friends. If that weren't bad enough, she grounded me right there until I could develop a better attitude about basketball and try harder—whatever that means."

  Janie was right; her mom had blown it. She had violated the terms of the contract, plain and simple. Janie was in no mood to talk things out rationally, so I suggested that I talk to her mother.

Elena and I talked about how disappointed all the parents were that the girls had lost the season championship in such a close game. As Elena thought about what she had said to Janie, she uttered, "Oh no, how could I have been so thoughtless?" Caught up in the emotion of the moment, Elena had acted without thinking. She was disappointed and unfortunately took it out on Janie. I asked Elena how she thought she could make this up to Janie. I knew that, like most parents of teenagers, Elena rarely apologized to Janie, but in this case I felt an honest apology was in order. Elena asked if she could let Janie know she was sorry right then and there in my office. When Janie came back in, Elena apologized and they patched things up. As Janie left she whispered, "Wow, Mom's never done anything like that. Maybe she can get the hang of this contract after all."

- **Anticipate lapses of interest.** Every so often, you or your teen may lose interest in the contract for several days, perhaps even a week. For example, you may forget to keep track of your teen's compliance. You may let up and follow the contract in a haphazard manner. If this happens, instead of beating yourself up for veering off track, concentrate on getting the contract going again.

- **Expect bad days.** Take it a day at a time. Expect bad days and good days. Acknowledge the good days and celebrate them with your teen. Don't dwell on the bad days. Avoid reminding your teen over and over again about how he goofed up. In fact, let it go. With your contract in effect, your teen will experience the consequences of goofing up by losing a privilege or not earning free time or credits. Usually the terms of the contract provide punishment enough. No constructive function is served by criticism and chastising; in fact, it will weaken the contract's effectiveness.

Every family has bad days. These are often caused by factors that have no direct bearing on the contract itself or the behavior of the parents. They just happen. The best you can do is to try to get through, and then past, these days. Let's look at how the Webers dealt with a bad day. Karen and Jesse Weber had been using a contract with their two sons, Neil, 14, and Joel, 12, for more than a week. The first week had gone fairly well and the boys seemed to enjoy earning and spending credits for following family rules and finishing schoolwork. Given their relative success, the Webers weren't ready for what became known as terrible Tuesday.

Although the Webers were hardly morning people, they usually were able to function well enough. Such was not the case on this particular Tuesday. Neil was grumpy and impossible from the moment his alarm went off. He even begged to stay home from school although he showed no signs of being sick. Joel couldn't resist and taunted Neil that he must have the math test flu. Neil blew up and insisted he really was ill. On top of this, Karen was anxious about a big presentation at work, wasn't buying Neil's act, and was losing her patience. Jesse found himself responding to this accelerating negativity by screaming at the boys to get in the car "right now or else," as it was time to leave for school. Neil rebutted with, "You guys are going to be sorry when I'm on my deathbed and the school nurse calls you to come get me."

When Karen picked the boys up after school, both were in bad moods. Karen tried what she could to cheer them up but to no avail. Neil had forgotten he was sick but couldn't shake his memory of the awful math test. He expressed his displeasure this way: "Not only did the math test stink, but that dorky genius Roy had to brag about how he aced it." Then Joel chimed in, "You think you had a bad day? I've got to do a project with Alicia and Rebecca. They are such jerks, always whispering to each other and laughing." "Poor Joel, he has to work with the girlie, girlies, work with the girlies, girlies," Neil teased. At that point the boys accelerated into a full fight complete with hurling things at one another.

Pulling off the road, Karen, composing herself as best she could, interrupted, "Cut that out right now, boys, that's enough. I'm sorry you had such bad days. If you don't stop this bickering and fighting, you're going to lose credits." Certain that his life was falling apart, Neil blurted out, "Like I care about those stupid babyish credits anyway." "Me, too," Joel added.

The boys continued to pick at one another for the rest of the day. Since neither parent was able to stop this behavior, they announced to Neil and Joel that they wouldn't be earning credits. Karen let them know that she was going to ignore them until they could get along. Jesse added that he hoped they'd be able to finish their homework so that they could stay up later and watch their favorite television show with him. Jesse's message seemed to hit home. Neil told Joel to lay off so he could get his work done. Joel retaliated with "Hey, you're the one who was bugging me" as he left the room to get started on his homework. Both boys finished their schoolwork. Jesse was not in the mood to watch television with his sons because of their earlier obnoxious behavior, but he did it anyway. According to their contracts, Neil and Joel had earned this privilege. However, Jesse did set a rule. He alerted the boys that if they started bickering, he'd turn off the television and they'd have to go to bed. This rule worked and all three watched the entire program together.

Using all their restraint and calming each other down, Karen and Jesse avoided a blowup with their boys. By offering each other support they were able to stay cool and stick with the contract. As we talked about terrible Tuesday, Jesse realized that on days with tests, especially math tests, Neil often fell apart and lashed out at his brother and parents. In a later chapter, we'll take a look at how Karen and Jesse figured out how to help Neil deal with this anxiety over tests. In addition, we'll take a look at how they worked with Joel when he got upset over having to work with girls on group projects.

The important thing to remember is not to revoke the contract no matter how fed up you get. If you do, you're left even more powerless.

HANDLING CONTRACT VIOLATIONS

By now you're certainly aware of the importance of following through with the terms of your contract. Although we've looked in general at limit testing and failure to comply with the contract, this section takes a further look at contract violations and how to deal with them. Contract infractions can range from minor lapses, e.g., your son coming home 10 minutes late, to major catastrophes, e.g., your daughter coming home three hours late and obviously intoxicated. The way you handle a violation should depend not only on the severity of the violation, but on the acute or chronic nature of the infraction as well. In addition, the way in which you find out about your teen's noncompliance is pertinent. Let's take a look at using your contract to curb violations. I recognize that, given the ingenuity and creativity of teenagers, these examples are not exhaustive, but hopefully the following situations will provide some guidelines to use when your teen fails to comply with his contract.

- **Confessing a rule infraction.** On rare occasions your teen may come to you and confess a transgression. Savor this opportunity to talk with your teen about what happened. If your teen willingly tells you about a mistake he made, it usually signals that he wants your support and help to avoid repeating the situation.

  Confessed first-time offenses are best treated by beginning with a matter-of-fact statement that your teen broke a rule and will be punished according to the terms of the contract. You should go on to acknowledge how much you appreciate your teen confiding in you about what happened. You can also let your teen know how difficult it must be for him to tell you about something he did wrong. A calm discussion of exactly what happened and how your teen feels about it is the best next step. You can follow this discussion with an exploration of different ways your teen could respond to this type of situation in the future.

  Margaret Bowles used this approach when her daughter Wendy confessed to smoking some cigarettes. Margaret let Wendy know that she had violated her contract and would have an earlier curfew for the next two weeks. Then Margaret added that she was proud of Wendy for being honest and asked if Wendy would like to talk about what happened. Wendy very much wanted to talk. She began, "It was stupid on my part and I didn't like the way it tasted. John was smoking and offered me a cigarette. Everyone else was smoking, so I went ahead and tried one. Even though I got dizzy and the cigarette smelled awful, I went ahead and finished it and even had a few puffs of Rachael's cigarette. I know it was a dumb thing to do." At this point Margaret and Wendy talked about how she could refuse in the future. In the first place, Wendy didn't like hanging out with John or Rachael because they always pushed her to do things she didn't want to do. Wendy decided to steer clear of John and Rachael. If she were offered a cigarette in the future, she'd say "No thank you" and leave the situation. Wendy confided to her mom that she knew she'd be teased about not wanting to smoke, but that, because she and her mom had talked, she felt better able to handle her classmates' jeers.

- **Getting caught in a lie.** It's much more typical for your teen to maintain his silence about committing a contract violation in hopes he'll get away with his crime because you wouldn't find out about it. Here's an example of how one of my clients reacted when she discovered that her son had lied to her about what he had done on the previous Saturday night.

  Georgia Upson had been using a contract successfully for several weeks and she was pleased with the progress her 14-year-old son, James, had made. So she was flabbergasted when she learned that he had lied to her about his activities on the previous Saturday. She felt she should address this situation as soon as possible. When James got home from school she asked him to sit down and listen because she had something very important to talk to him about. James was terrified.

What had he done now, he asked himself. Could his mom have found out about that little escapade last weekend? Who could have told her?

His mom got right to the point, "James, I found out that you lied to me and that you didn't stay at Neil's house but sneaked out and went to Gina's house when her parents weren't home. I consider that a serious violation of our agreement, and to be honest I'm not feeling like I trust you very much right now. You'll be grounded for the next two weeks on both weekend nights. In addition to that, I think we need to talk about what happened and how you can prevent it from happening again. I'd like you to tell me what happened."

Hoping to sidetrack his mom, James rattled off these questions: "Who ratted on me? The finks. Does Neil's mom know? Are you going to tell her? Neil will kill me if his mom finds out. Does Dad know? What's he going to do to me?"

Unfazed by his ploy, Georgia restated her original question, "James, what happened?"

Feeling boxed in, James attempted to defend himself. "Well, it wasn't my fault, and it wasn't my idea. Neil came up with a plan to tell his mom that we were going to the movie because it was just too boring at his house and we'd only be gone for a couple of hours. She dropped us off at the movie. We went into the theater, waited for her to leave, and then walked to Gina's house. A few other kids were there but it was even more boring than Neil's house. So we walked around for a while and then went back to the movie theater. We were there when Neil's dad came to pick us up. Nothing happened. What's the big deal?"

In the past, Georgia might have exploded with a barrage of zingers at James's poor judgment; however, this time she simply responded, "Thank you for telling me the truth. I know that wasn't easy. I consider what you did seriously wrong for a number of reasons. I'll try to review them as calmly as possible and I'd like you to listen and not interrupt me. You'll have your turn when I'm finished. Can you agree to that?" If he had refused, Georgia would have said something like, "Then go to your room until you're ready to listen. I won't forget about this and until we finish our talk, you're restricted except for school, so you might as well listen to me and get it over with." But James didn't refuse.

Georgia continued, "You lied to me about where you were and what you did. We've been doing pretty well trusting one another, but lying always undermines trust. You'll have to earn it back. Although nothing happened, a lot *could* have. I know you and Neil are good kids who don't get in trouble, but being at Gina's house when her parents weren't home and when we didn't know you were there could have gotten you in a lot of trouble. And walking around in the dark on a weekend night, just the two of you, well, that's not a good idea. Here's the bottom line. Since nothing happened and no one was hurt, I won't tell Neil's mother this time. However, if I find out that Neil and you pull one of these stunts in the future, I will tell his mother and you will not be allowed to see him for one month except at school. I'll give you the choice of telling Neil about this rule yourself or he can come over here and the three of us can talk."

James decided he'd handle Neil on his own. Later that week he spoke with Neil about how he'd been grounded for lying to his parents. As it turned out, Neil's dad had found out what happened and had grounded Neil as well. Although both James and Neil felt that their parents were blowing things way out of proportion, they reluctantly agreed not to sneak over to friends' houses and to be honest with their parents about where they were going.

James's and Neil's parents did what they did because they wanted to send a message loud and clear that lying is unacceptable. They also felt that, at 14, their sons weren't mature enough to be making decisions about how to spend their Saturday nights on their own. Their boys clearly still needed their parents' OK.

Minor Infractions

I consider contract violations such as coming home a few minutes late, forgetting to call in on schedule, being late to school, or doing poorly on a quiz or test minor infractions. The first time any of these occur, your best bet is to issue a warning that further offenses will result in an earlier curfew. If that isn't enough to turn your teen's behavior around, a one- or two-night grounding may do the trick.

Major Infractions

I consider engaging in prohibited activities such as smoking, drinking, or using drugs major infractions. Promiscuity, stealing, vandalism, cheating, sneaking out, driving without permission, harassing others, or getting into a fight rank as major infractions as well. Driving after drinking and/or riding with someone who's been drinking are also major violations. When you find out about a first-time major violation, here's how I'd suggest you handle it.

- **Do not go ballistic.** Teens often are tempted by peers to experiment and try out prohibited behaviors such as smoking, drinking alcohol, or trying marijuana. They may also do things that start out silly and then morph into major violations. For example, in a group setting it's easy for teens to turn an innocent prank such as toilet papering someone's front yard into destruction of property and vandalism. Keep in mind that teens are curious. They may want to try something just to see how it feels. Doing something that's prohibited once doesn't mean your teen will make it a lifelong habit.

- **Calmly state the violation and the consequence.** In an objective and matter-of-fact manner, let your teen know what he did that was wrong. I recommend you invoke a weekend of grounding as a consequence for your teen's misbehavior.

- **Make it clear that you don't want this violation to happen again.** Let your teen know that you're disappointed in what she did. Ask her if she understands why you're upset. If she does, take a positive tack and share your belief that your teen won't do it again. Add that we all make mistakes and hopefully learn from them. If she doesn't understand, tell her why you consider her actions wrong, but don't insist that she agree with your assessment.

- **Talk about preventing a repeat of the major violation.** Discuss with your teen what steps could have been taken to alter the outcome. If he's interested in this exercise, that's great. Together, explore how he could handle a similar situation in the future. If your teen doesn't understand what the big deal is, don't waste your time trying to convince him that he committed a major violation or trying to get him to admit to wrongdoing. Instead, make it clear that no matter what his perspective is concerning his behavior, you believe what he did was wrong and you don't want him to do it again.

- **Outline the punishments that will be given if the violation recurs.** These punishments can include additional grounding for a longer period of time, loss of driving privileges, and/or no contact with friends for a certain period of time. You can also let your teen know that if she misbehaves again, you'll set up a meeting with her and her friends and let them know you're aware of what they're doing. Inform them that if they're able to mend their ways immediately, you won't tell their parents; however, if they goof up, you'll call a meeting of their parents. By using these steps you're giving your teen and her friends a chance to stop on their own.

- **If in spite of your punishments the major violations continue to occur, consider getting outside professional help.** If your teen seems oblivious to accelerating punishments and continues to participate in prohibited behaviors, you should explore getting extra help. Usually, in this kind of situation you don't have enough power to change your teen's behavior. You're most likely emotionally enmeshed.

  Sometimes with chronic, serious contract violations, you may need outside help in determining how to effectively deal with your teen's problem behavior. A later chapter deals in detail with situations in which you need to bring in the big guns. If your teen displays chronic or serious antisocial behaviors, is sexually promiscuous, and/or has a substance abuse problem, get help immediately. Talking about how your teen can change is not enough. Find an agent of change.

It's always preferable to prevent major contract violations. One way to do this is to help your teen learn to take personal responsibility for his behavior. The next part of this book addresses personal responsibility by taking you through programs on clarifying values and solving problems. So let's get started learning how to help your teen become accountable for his behavior.

II

Teaching Personal Responsibility

An important function of your contract is that it provides your teen with an *external* structure. By offering rewards and punishments, this structure motivates her to act responsibly and follow safety, school, and family rules. In this chapter, we'll explore how you can help your teen develop her own *internal* structure. First we'll look at tips on helping your teen clarify her values. Then we'll turn our attention to steps your teen can take to solve her own problems.

CLARIFYING VALUES

Your teen needs encouragement to help him clarify and internalize the values and standards upon which responsible rule-driven behavior is based. The goal of this process is to help your teen use good judgment, make good decisions, and behave responsibly on his own.

Because your ability to communicate effectively with your teen is a prerequisite to the values-clarification process, let's quickly review the communication techniques you've learned so far.

Continue to Communicate with Your Teen

If you've followed along with the steps in this book you've already made some big strides in improving communication.

As you review the following tips, take a moment to assess how well you're following them. If you feel you need additional practice with them before embarking on the task at hand, take as much time as you need to feel comfortable with them. Let's take a quick look at some of the communication-building techniques you may have tried out with your teen.

- **Say positive things.** As you began this book, your first task was to say something nice to each family member every day. Future projects encouraged you to spend unstructured time with your teen during which you listened attentively and gave support rather than criticizing or cross-examining.

- **Listen patiently and be supportive.** You've also been asked to be quietly available and ready to listen patiently when and if your teen wants to talk. I've recommended that you give your teen a chance to tell you what happened rather than jumping to conclusions or assuming the worst case. I've suggested you ask general, nonthreatening, interested questions and then wait for an answer rather than being accusatory.

- **Avoid using zingers.** Together we've reviewed guidelines to help you defuse emotionally loaded words (zingers) that your teen uses to set you off. You've also considered alternatives to using these trigger words yourself.

- **Don't be judgmental.** You've also been asked to avoid lecturing as well as branding your teen with negative, generalized, nonspecific characterizations such as immaturity, irresponsibility, disrespect, and/or untrustworthiness. You've been instructed to replace these negatively charged barbs with a calm, nonthreatening statement about the specific consequences for his/her transgression.

- **Continue your unstructured, nonstressed talk times.** Never abandon these times as they allow you and your teen to enjoy each other without any demand characteristics. These interchanges are essential to your ongoing relationship with your teen. Don't stop offering a supportive, noncritical ear as you listen to your teen tell you about the day's events or whatever else he wants to talk about. Enjoy sharing a joke or a silly conversation about nothing. By being together and acknowledging each other in positive and empowering ways, you're strengthening your bond with your teen. Let's take a look at how you can use a portion of this talk time to explore values on an ongoing basis.

Clarifying Your Own Values

Before you can help your teen clarify his values, you need to make sure you're clear about your own. The rules and punishments you are using in your contract are based on your values; even so, at this juncture it's a good idea to look even more carefully at your own values and how they influence the standards you have for your teen. Most parents do not want their teens to cheat, lie, steal, take drugs, smoke cigarettes, drink alcohol, or hang with the wrong crowd. Parents are not as likely to be in total agreement about acceptable sexual behavior, but, whatever their views, most parents don't condone promiscuity. They want their teen protected from disease and unwanted pregnancy. Obviously parents should prohibit physical violence of any kind. They should also prohibit verbal abuse such as mean-spirited teasing, bullying, or harassing younger or less powerful children, name calling, and making any kind of prejudicial remarks or ethnic slurs.

As you think about your values, ask yourself *why* you believe what you believe. Try to go beyond such reasons as "it's right" or "it's wrong." For one thing, using these short answers will turn your teen off pronto. Ask yourself "*why* do I think it's right or wrong?"

The Bedrock of Values

An underlying precept of values and morals is respecting the rights of self and others. Such a lofty notion must be translated into everyday behavior to give it meaning and life. For example, respecting the rights of one's self can be the basis for saying no to harmful behavior whether it's physical (smoking, drinking, drugs) or emotional (refusing to tolerate verbal abuse from peers). Showing empathy for others and respecting differences in beliefs, customs, and religions also reflects respecting the rights of others.

Helping Your Teen Develop Values

All parents want their teens to have strong values, but how does this happen? Lecturing your teen is tempting but usually ineffective. Giving teens complete freedom to make their own choices is most often a disaster. It's easy to endorse values in the abstract while not always following them in one's personal life. As a parent, one of your most important responsibilities is bringing values into your teen's daily life. Let's look at some ways you can do this.

- **Be a role model for your teen.** Are you practicing what you preach? Are you charitable toward others? Do you tell the truth? Do you refrain from illegal activities? Are you a good friend? Do you follow through on your word? Even though you may think your teen isn't paying attention, your teen is watching you and what you do. You don't have to be perfect, but if you violate your own standards, what can you expect of your teen? When you feel like you acted in a manner that was inconsistent with your standards, I'd advise you to discuss this with your teen. If you encounter a situation in which acting morally seems like a gray area, talk about this as well.

- **Relate values to ongoing events.** In general, seize any opportunity to talk with your teen about values. When you begin this process, pick relatively neutral subjects. In other words, don't start out with hot topics such as sex or drugs. Refrain from being alarmist as well. Overly emotional responses and pronouncements will either turn your teen off or incite her to argue the opposite viewpoint.

  For example, let's say you saw lots of teens smoking in the high school parking lot. When you discuss this with your teen, don't pass judgment or overreact. Avoid pronouncements such as, "Teenagers today are out of control and killing themselves with cigarettes. What morons. Don't they know they're ruining their health?" Instead, try beginning your conversation with something like, "I was surprised by all the kids I saw smoking in the parking lot today. Does that happen a lot? Does anyone at school do anything about it? I guess those kids haven't paid much attention to the anti-smoking program at school. What do you think?"

- **Discuss news or entertainment.** Begin with neutral topics. The most nonthreatening situation is often when you and your teen have listened to or watched something together. You can follow this up by asking your teen a question about what you just experienced. Encourage open, free-flowing discussions without judgment or criticism. Keep your discussion down to earth, specific, topical, and interesting. You may disagree with your teen. If so, try to talk about your point of view calmly and factually.

Some parents don't want to do take this step, which is a real shame. Instead of proactively taking on the task of values clarification, too many parents wait until their teen doesn't live up to their standards and react with a punishment. Continual interchanges between parents and teens help teens form meaningful, internalized values and over time use them as a basis for their decisions.

As you and your teen get comfortable sharing your viewpoints, you can move into more volatile areas, such as professional athletes' ethics and treatment of women; movies' depiction of violence and drugs; and television's treatment of teenage sexuality. Anything is fair game.

For example, when you and your teen finish watching a teen drama such as *Dawson's Creek*, you might ask her opinion about what happened between two characters: "What do you think Sheila should have done when John tried to kiss her? Do you think Sheila wanted him to kiss her? Why did she let him kiss her?" Encourage a give-and-take discussion that is nonjudgmental. Don't be confrontational.

- **Use real-life situations.** You can also bring up a situation that you and your teen experienced together. I remember driving to soccer practice when one of my son Sean's teammates (I'll call him Ralph) was talking disparagingly about a certain ethnic group. After we dropped this teammate off, I let Sean know how upset

Ralph's comments had made me. I then added, "I thought about saying something but I didn't, which makes me mad at myself. I guess I rationalized that he hears words like that at home all the time from his parents. I've heard them say that to me and in front of him, so I figured my comments would just fall on deaf ears. What did you think about the situation?" We talked for a while about the pluses and minuses of confronting others in this type of situation and decided there were no hard and fast rules. We agreed that we didn't like Ralph's behavior but felt that confronting him in the car wouldn't accomplish much.

Another means of bringing up values is for you to describe a situation you encountered and talk with your teen about it. Again, your discussion should be focused on exploring the values involved. For example, Heidi Furrow shared this situation with her daughter Nancy. "When I dropped off the PTA schedule at school, I saw a number of kids bullying and teasing a younger boy who was crying. You know how I feel about teasing. I told them to stop it right now. I also told the lunch attendant what I had seen. Does that sound like ratting to you?" By talking about what happened Nancy decided that because the younger children were being abused she didn't think what her mom had done was ratting.

- **Encourage appreciating the needs of others.** How do you encourage a teen who is caught up in his own life and problems to think about the needs of others? The best way to help your teen acquire an appreciation for the needs and concerns of others is direct involvement in a hands-on experience helping others. This can take many forms including baby-sitting, coaching, tutoring younger children, or working with the elderly. Don't prescribe or demand a specific community service, rather help your teen choose activities that interest him. Encourage him to give whatever he chooses a try for at least a month or two. Again, be available to listen to whatever he has to say about his experience. Do not include community service as a behavior that is rewarded on your teen's contract. In time the intrinsic reward of helping others should be reward and incentive enough for him to continue providing his community service.

As you work with your teen and help him clarify his values, you may also want to have discussions about the temptations he'll face. Let him know that you understand the peer pressure he's likely to encounter to do something he knows he's not supposed to do—something that's not in keeping with his values. Encourage him to see that if he's had the opportunity to think through various responses he has a better chance of standing up for himself. Helping your teen plan out how he'll handle difficult situations falls under the heading of problem solving, which we'll explore next.

SOLVING PROBLEMS

Values are the fundamental building blocks of behavior and should be a guiding force in how problems are solved. Solving problems can help teens translate values into pragmatic action.

Although mastering problem solving is often a journey down a rocky road, the bumps and detours are generally worth the end result. In this chapter you'll learn a step-by-step problem-solving method that you and your teen can work through together as you tackle her problems. As your teen learns how to solve her own problems, she'll experience as newfound control over her behavior and become empowered to make good decisions on her own. When you engage your teen in the problem-solving process, use these general guidelines.

Guidelines

- **Work together.** Your teen should be an active participant in solving her problems. Go at her pace, respect
her timetable, take a break as needed, and stop whenever she wants to. Encourage her to engage in the reasoning process and make her own decisions. Don't try
to fix her problems; instead guide and consult her as
she does the work.

- **Go slowly.** Although diving right in and solving a big
problem all in one sitting is tempting, a one-time-only
stab at a problem usually is doomed to failure because
everyone gets overwhelmed by the magnitude of the
task and gives up. An ongoing dialogue is the only
realistic chance you have. Sorting thorough conflict-
laden, confusing areas is a never-ending process that
requires a step-by-step approach punctuated by
"patience breaks"—lasting from minutes to days—
where each participant regroups, gathers additional
data, and gains new perspective.

- **Make sure it's a good time for your teen and for you.**
When talking to teens about problems, keep in mind
that parents and teens sometimes exist on different
wavelengths and that parents often pick the worst possible times to try and work something out. It's not so
much that teens don't want to talk about these things,
it's just that they want to talk about them at their own
pace when they feel in the mood. Gentle introductions
and going slowly are really important. If your first
attempt fails, don't give up. These are complicated and
emotionally charged areas and deserve prolonged time
and attention. Teens need permission to tell their parents when the conversation is stressing them out, and
parents should do the same. Take your time.

You may also be caught at a bad time. Sometimes as much as we may want to listen well, we're just too tired or too distracted to pay attention. When this happens to you, I recommend that you acknowledge your state of mind. You might say something like, "I am so wiped out I can't talk or even listen very attentively now. I want to hear what happened, but could it wait just a bit?" If you pretend you're listening, you may find it hard to commiserate with your teen's problems. You may even overreact, lose your temper, and come down on your teen with an explosive comment like, "You think that's bad? Guess what happened to *me* today?"

In time your teen may even stop what he's talking about and ask you if you had a bad day and if you'd like to talk about it!

Getting Started

- **Coping with complaints.** Before you introduce the steps of the problem-solving process, you should make sure your teen is already comfortable complaining about what's bothering him. During talk times, your teen is likely to let off steam from time to time. In response to his complaints about his day, you listen and provide support. You may also let your teen know that, if you were in his situation, you'd be upset, confused, and frustrated too, or that you understand these feelings.

- **Putting a positive spin on the day.** I recommend that you encourage your teen to look on the bright side of life. There are a number of ways of doing this. For example, after you've given your teen time to complain, you might say something like, "Sounds like a yucky day. Did anything good happen?" If your teen is stumped and unable to come up with anything positive, you might add, "Sometimes when I've had a horrible day I challenge myself to think of one good thing that happened. I may have to get really creative or stretch things but I can usually come up with a good thing or at least a neutral thing. Maybe that sounds silly to you, but it helps cheer me up." Some parents also use a system in which their teen rates her day on a 1 to 10 scale with 1 being the worst and 10 being the best.

The ability to differentiate the positive aspects of the day from the negative ones and keep a more upbeat perspective of things will help your teen become a more motivated problem solver.

Steps of Problem Solving

The problem-solving process you'll be learning about explores the possibility that your teen can improve a problem situation. This is a learned concept. It is not a point of view that automatically develops as a child matures socially or intellectually. In fact, there are many adults who have few if any problem solving skills. It's up to you, the parent, to make sure your teen masters the steps of problem solving.

Make the Transition from Listening to Asking If Your Teen Is Upset. Although some teens will come right out and tell you they have a problem they want your help to solve, that is the exception, not the rule. In most cases, you'll be transitioning from listening to your teen's complaints to implementing the steps of problem solving. To begin the problem-solving process, after a certain amount of ranting, commiserate with your teen about the situation. You might let her know that you would find the circumstances difficult as well.

Spend Time Talking About What's Upsetting Your Teen. As always, diplomacy and very careful wording are important here. Say something general, such as, "It sounds like you're upset. I'm sorry you're upset. Do you feel like talking about it?" This gives her an opportunity to share what's upsetting her if she wants to.

Try not to say things that minimize the importance of the problem. Avoid comments such as "That doesn't sound like a problem to me," "It's a part of life; you'll have many worse problems," or "I'm surprised you can't figure out how to solve that." Don't supply her with your take on what the solution to her problem should be. For example, if she's concerned about a poor grade, refrain from stating something like, "This wouldn't have happened if only you had studied harder and not stayed out so late."

If you're reading between the lines and think something might be troubling your teen, proceed very gently. You might ask, "Are you OK? You seem a little down. I was wondering if anything was bothering you."

If your teen is unaccustomed to inquiries of this type, he may respond as though you're accusing him of something. Again, tread carefully. "Well, you seem upset about school and friends. I haven't seen Joyce for a long time. Didn't you hang out with her?"

If you've hit the nail on the head, don't be surprised to hear, "Joyce is a total flake and I don't want to talk about her."

Accept Your Teen's Request Not to Talk Any More. Your teen may not be ready to talk about whatever is troubling her. If this is the case, you can add, "OK. I hope you feel like you can tell me if something's bothering you. I care about you. If something's troubling you, please let me know. I won't get mad at you." This is tricky ground—you have to mean it. You may not agree with what your teen did; in fact, you may not approve of what is upsetting your teen. You may be disappointed to find out that the problem involves a behavior that upsets you. For example, your teen might tell you, "Joyce is such a goody-goody. She wouldn't give me the answers to the English test. What are friends for?" As angry as this may make you, try not to blow up because if you do you've lost your chance to help her work out her problem. Although you may initially strike out, don't be surprised if your teen brings up Joyce the flake at a later time and wants to talk about her.

Sometimes recognition is all your teen wants or is ready to handle. If he says, "No I don't want to talk about it anymore," say "That's OK. If you feel like talking about it later, I'll be glad to listen." Do not pry for details, and do not badger your teen to tell you more. If he's said something that's upset you and you're worried about his safety, calmly let him know that and ask for reassurance that there's no threat involved. You may want to say something like, "I won't get mad, but if this is serious I need to know."

Get Some Details About What Happens. If and when your teen is willing to discuss it, help her talk about what's troubling her. Help her describe what happens, how she acts when the problem happens. She may not have thought about what she does, only what the other people do.

She may answer with an emotional, general statement. If so, it's your job to assist her in clarifying what she means and to come up with some specifics. For example, you might ask what she means when she makes a general comment such as "Everyone hates me," "Boys stink," "I hate school," or "I can't stand it anymore."

Come Up with a Plan of Action. If and when your teen is ready to consider possible ways of solving his problem, here are some options for you to keep in mind.

- **Don't try to fix things yourself.** No matter how tempting it might seem, do not solve the problem on your own. This technique turns your teen off and doesn't help him learn the skills necessary to solve his own problems.

- **Do nothing.** For those infrequent, unavoidable, silly things that happen, doing nothing and trying to forget about it usually makes the best solution. For example, when your teen experiences embarrassing moments in front of friends or classmates, such as spilling his lunch tray all over himself in the cafeteria or tripping over his shoelaces in gym class, there's not much you can do but encourage him to laugh it off. Sometimes it can help if you have a story about how you did something similar when you were a teen. My teens loved the story of my first big formal dance at which my crinoline slip fell to the floor when I was dancing with a boy I had a crush on. Mortified, I stepped out of my slip, gathered it up and took it to the ladies room.

- **Give it time.** Some problems—particularly those that involve disagreements among friends—need time to take care of themselves. Teenagers, especially girls, are notorious for being best friends one day, mortal enemies the next, and then best friends again. If your teen is complaining about a problem with a friend repeatedly and she wants to do something about it, that's another matter. You and your teen can consider some of the plans of action listed below.

- **Ignore, leave, and/or avoid unchangeable situations.** Some situations your teen encounters are for all practical purposes unchangeable and/or unavoidable. In such cases, the best course of action your teen can take is to try to ignore, leave, or avoid the unchangeable situations. If your teen is bullied by older children or teased by the popular kids, fighting back is unlikely to get him anywhere. He's much better off avoiding the perpetrators and seeking out same-age friends who are nice to him. By talking with your teen about who the nice kids at school are and how he might meet them, you can help him develop some relationships that are good for him.

- **Explore taking action.** You can always ask if your teen would like to try to make things better. He may not have decided or he may believe there is nothing he can do. If your teen asks for your input, you can say something empathetic and supportive. For example, if your teen is tired of being teased by Matt, who is a bully, you might offer your observation by saying, "It sounds like Matt makes you really angry when he makes fun of you. Is there any way you could think of to change this situation?" Encourage your teen to think about the following types of options. Stay clear of Matt. Avoid Matt. Ignore him. Count to 10. The chances of Matt changing his behavior are remote, so discourage solutions such as asking Matt to stop it. You may also want to talk about the reasons for Matt's meanness. Sometimes it helps teens to recognize that the teaser or name caller is usually an unhappy, angry person taking it out on others.

- **Suggest calming down.** What teenager doesn't fly off the handle from time to time and blow up at a friend, a sibling, or a parent? Certainly your teen needs a chance to cool off and calm down before she does anything else. Trying to force an apology out of an angry teen won't work—it will even make matters worse. In fact, badgering your teen to say "I'm sorry" is counterproductive in most cases. Teens who are forced to say they're sorry rarely mean it, which makes parents even madder. As a parent, try to take the high road. Acknowledge that you got pretty upset and that you'd like to patch things up and start from the beginning. This allows your teen to save face but also alerts her that you're expecting her to change her behavior. If your teen is angry all the time, you may want to consider getting counseling that focuses on anger management. We look more at this option in the following chapter.

- **Encourage being better prepared.** Teens generally don't like to admit that if they had prepared more for things, especially school tasks, they could do better. However, increased efforts at preparing usually result in less anxiety and improved performance in school. In a previous chapter we met the Weber family and their sons, Neil, 14, who came unglued before each math test, and Joel, 12, who dreaded doing group projects especially if girls were involved. Building on their contract, the boys' parents, Karen and Jesse, used the problem-solving steps you just read about to help their sons address these problems.

  Rather than concentrating on Neil's test performance and his grades, his parents worked with him to improve his basic math skills. They also talked with him about how math was easy for some of his classmates but that he excelled in other subjects, such as science and athletics. They discussed how he felt when his classmate Roger bragged about his math scores. Neil said it made him and rest of the class feel stupid. He added that no one liked Roger because he was such a braggart. With help from Neil's math teacher, and with Neil's agreement, his parents began giving him practice tests at home. As Neil got more comfortable taking tests at home, he was able to relax at school as well. And as he told his parents, being able to ignore Mr. Know-It-All Roger was the best part.

Try New Experiences. Karen and Jesse Weber also used problem solving to help Joel with his dread of group projects, especially when girls were involved. First they offered him a special incentive for being involved in the current group project. If Joel followed through with the project, he could earn a computer game he wanted. They made sure to review the project with him and each task he was assigned. They encouraged the group to meet from time to time at their house to keep track of the progress everyone was making. As Joel got to know his group members, he realized they weren't as bad and stuck up as he had thought. In fact, they were rather shy just like he was. Over time Joel quit complaining about the group and actually joined in.

Make the Most After the Fact. There are some problems that neither your teen nor you can do anything about because they've happened and the consequence has been determined before you ever hear about it. For example, at my home we were faced with this situation when my son Mike was in seventh grade. I'll never forget the look of terror on his face as he told me that he had been suspended from school for a day. Having no idea what horrible crime my normally shy, reticent son had committed, I think I said something like, "That's awful. I'm sorry. What happened?" and prepared myself for the worst.

Relentlessly taunted by Kate, a fellow student in his industrial arts class, Mike snapped and tossed his safety goggles at her as he yelled, "Shut up." Never a pitching prodigy, Mike's goggles missed Kate altogether, instead grazing big, strong Tom's knee before crashing to the ground. Unfortunate wild pitch. Lunging toward Mike, Tom slugged him in the stomach. The outcome: Mike and Tom were suspended for one day. Mike apologized to Kate, the innocent victim, who avoided punishment completely. As stupid as I thought this whole situation was and as unfair as I thought the punishment was, I didn't intervene. Mike had to take the consequences of his actions and learn from experience.

We did however, spend time talking about how Mike's impulsive actions could have caused harm. We discussed ways in which to prevent this situation from happening in the future. Mike came up with different ways to behave. And we made up some rules together, such as, "Never throw goggles or anything else, no matter what," and "Stay away from/tune out Tom and Kate." Mike realized he'd made a mistake and paid the consequence. All he could do was make sure a situation like this never happened again.

Acknowledge a Lifelong Process. Solving problems is an ongoing, never-ending process. Being able to look at one's problems and try out solutions is very empowering and greatly increases the odds that your teen will act in a personally responsible manner.

Exploring Aspirations

What do you want to be when you grow up? Teens aren't supposed to know the answer to this question during middle school or high school. Adolescence is a great time to try on different hats. For example, many high schools offer their students a chance to check out what it's like to be an actor, a journalist, an athlete, an artist, and/or a politician. Don't expect your teen to know what she wants to do. (After all, aren't most of us still asking ourselves the same question?) If she's on the right track don't put her under a microscope. Don't expect her to be what you are or what you wish you were. Be honest about this to yourself. If you can talk about future aspirations without putting pressure on your teen it can be an eye-opening and very meaningful conversation. Give your teen free rein to talk about all kinds of things he'd like to be and do. Don't freak out if he mentions bungee jumping, fire fighting, sword swallowing, or even becoming an attorney. It's healthy to explore all the options and how great for your teen to be able to do so with her parents.

In middle school don't be surprised if your teen goes from one interest to another. One year she may play soccer, take cello lessons, and be interested in the school newspaper. The next year she may be involved with basketball, pottery, and drama. As your teen approaches high school, her interests may solidify a bit. She may concentrate on only one or two activities. Whatever her druthers, celebrate her interests and enjoy the ride. She'll have to become serious and focused soon enough.

PART V

TAKING STOCK, GETTING HELP, AND LOOKING AHEAD

12

Evaluating the Progress Your Teen Has Made

After you've successfully used the contract for three or four months, it's time to take stock of your teen's progress. Ask yourself each of the questions that follow. As you're answering, keep in mind that some of the behavior changes described can take a long time. So if they haven't happened for your teen yet, don't be discouraged. You need to give your contract more time.

IS YOUR TEEN DOING A BETTER JOB OF FOLLOWING THE RULES?

Since it's easy to forget what your teen's behavior was like before, you may want to remind yourself by taking a look at your contract from the first week. Is your teen acting the way you want more often? Is he following the rules and earning points and enjoying activities?

Let's see what happened when my clients Elaine and George Brown compared their 14-year-old son, Derek's, behavior then and now.

As Elaine and George Brown looked over Derek's first contract, they couldn't help but smile. In the last eight weeks Derek had really improved on all fronts, most notably in his attitude toward his parents. Before Elaine and George began the contract, if they asked Derek to help with the dishes or straighten up his room, he ignored them or promised to do it later. Occasionally, if they kept begging him, he'd make a half-hearted attempt by taking his plate and glass to the sink and then make a beeline for the television. Fortunately the prospect of earning rewards changed Derek's approach to helping out. With points on the line, he usually did what his parents asked and sometimes even volunteered to help.

Elaine, George, and I talked about how important it was that they had quit nagging Derek about everything they wanted him to do and instead supplied him with incentives. With this change, Derek no longer experienced his parents as negative and badgering. Instead he saw them as the bearers of good news—the source of positive comments and rewards. Instead of avoiding Elaine and George, Derek started to seek them out.

IS YOUR TEEN OPENING UP AND TALKING WITH YOU?

By encouraging your teen to talk and listen, she should be opening up and confiding in you more. Think about recent talk times you've spent with your teen. Are the two of you able to talk about her positive and negative feelings and experiences? Let's see how my clients the Judds used their talk time to encourage their daughter Carrie to talk to them.

Eleven-year-old Carrie, the ever silent one, was finally open-ing up to her parents, Curt and Kathy. Ever since they had stopped interrogating her every day about what happened at middle school and instead begun listening to her, Carrie had responded by sharing her day. On a recent day, Carrie had shared her excitement about Janet, a new friend, and the fun they'd had planning the outfits they'd wear to the school dance. When Carrie asked her mom if she could have Janet over before the dance to get ready, Kathy was quick to say, "Of course." Curt and Kathy were very pleased that they were beginning to communicate with Carrie and that she seemed to enjoy rattling on about school and her friends.

Curt, Kathy, and I talked about how this change in Carrie had come about largely because they had stopped interrupting her, pestering her, and criticizing her and instead started show-ing their concern, waiting until she felt like talking, and pro-viding a friendly ear. This environment was just what Carrie needed to open up and begin sharing with her parents.

IS YOUR FAMILY ENJOYING EACH OTHER MORE?

Think back to how your family interacted before the contract and compare that to what it's like when you're together now. Are there fewer arguments and fights? Does your family do more together now than they used to? Let's see how using a contract game helped my clients the Sipes start doing things together again.

"Dinner out with Ellen? Am I hearing correctly?" Ellen's grandmother, Shirley, wondered. She wasn't used to being in the same room with Ellen for more than five minutes, let alone going out to dinner with Ellen and her parents. Ellen had such a bad attitude that her parents had stopped trying to do any-thing as a family. Had something changed? Was Ellen over her bad attitude? Shirley asked herself. As it turned out Ellen's parents had been using a contract with Ellen for a month and had seen such improvement that they were willing to try a family dinner out complete with Grandma. Ellen's parents alerted Ellen ahead of time and planned the dinner so that it wouldn't interfere with her schedule. Ellen didn't offer any resistance because after dinner she got to go to the birthday party of one of her best friends. Her parents and grandmother couldn't help but notice that Ellen was surprisingly pleasant. Because Ellen had something to look forward to, it was much easier for her to get along with everyone for a few hours.

Is Your Teen Putting Forth More Effort?

By encouraging small steps of progress with her schoolwork, you should be helping your teen put forth additional effort. Because your support makes your teen feel like she can succeed, she isn't as likely to give up. Watch your teen when she's doing her schoolwork and see how long she's able to stick with it. Is she doing better than she did before you started using your contract? Is she able to concentrate on her homework? Is she trying at school? Let's see how rewarding short time periods helped my clients the Howards encourage their son to do his school assignments.

Patrick Howard, 14, always started his homework with a burst of enthusiasm. But then after a few minutes, he'd fizzle out, become distracted, and start daydreaming. Nagging him didn't help nor did long lectures on why he should do his homework. However, once his parents, Natalie and Trevor, started rewarding Patrick for short study periods, he got much better about sitting down and doing his assignments. As he explained to his parents, even though sometimes the work was hard, it was worth the effort because it felt good to get his work done and to get a reward.

When Natalie, Trevor, and I talked about Patrick's improvement, they were especially surprised by how proud Patrick was of getting his work done. Patrick almost always grinned with satisfaction, his father reported. Patrick's parents wanted to make sure it was OK to make a big deal of Patrick's success and to savor every moment of his pleasure. I reassured them that when it comes to homework, it's almost impossible for parents to be too enthusiastic, no matter what their teen's age is, and that in addition to giving Patrick a reward, they should continue letting Patrick know how pleased they were.

Has Your Teen's Self-Esteem Improved?

Lots of things that happen when your teen is involved in a contract help contribute to her feeling good about herself. Most important, when you acknowledge your teen's good behavior, she will begin to feel better about herself. Teens who hear about the good things they do instead of the bad learn to believe in themselves. They gradually recognize that they can do worthwhile things—that they're not always messing up. As they get used to their parents saying good things to them, they start saying good things to themselves. Let's see how Amy, the 15-year-old daughter of Tammy and Jim Easton, reacted to positive comments from her parents.

The first time 15-year-old Amy Easton and I talked, she made it clear that she felt as though the whole world was against her and that she couldn't do anything right. What made it worse, she told me, was that her younger sister Julie was "perfect." No one ever yelled at her or criticized her. But the moment Amy did even the littlest thing wrong, boom, her parents were all over her case.

Before her contract, Amy saw herself in negative terms and felt pretty bad about herself. But once her parents started using a contract and stopped using zingers, their praise and encouragement made Amy feel better about herself. The positive feedback she was getting from her parents helped Amy acknowledge the good things she did, such as coming home on time, finishing her schoolwork, and helping out when asked. After several months of using a contract, Amy confided in me that she felt better because she could get things done. As a plus she added that both her parents had undergone a personality transformation and become much less creepy to be around.

Does Your Teen Have His Anger Under Control?

Over time, using your contract should help your teen stay in control when he's upset. Hopefully, you've taught your teen different ways to cool off when he's angry. He should be better at calming down and less likely to overreact to situations. In addition, your discipline techniques like earlier curfew and grounding should have encouraged your teen to think before acting impulsively. Let's see how using a combination of providing rewards for good behavior at school and earlier curfews and grounding for fighting helped Jack and Denise Holden's son Greg cut down on his fighting at school.

After being involved with his contract for six weeks, Greg, 16, told me how sick he was of being punished for fighting at school. He felt it was totally unfair because most of the time he didn't even start the fight and was in his words "only protecting himself." But his parents didn't care who was at fault. If Greg got in a fight they reduced his curfew by one hour for the rest of the week and on the weekend. If he got in another fight during the week he was grounded for one weekend night. What really bugged him as well was that his parents always found out about his fights. And to make matters worse, his parents had set up a rule that he had to go one month without a fight before he could start driving lessons. At this point Greg wanted to stop fighting because it just got him in trouble. It wasn't worth it. We talked about what Greg could do in the future to stop fighting. Together we came up with the following ideas. Greg should avoid the other boys that he got in fights with whenever possible. He needed a response to give them when they taunted him to fight. He needed to be ready to take off if they initiated a fight. He had to decide if he could tolerate being verbally abused by the boys. Could he walk away if they called him a chicken, a sissy, or a wimp? Greg wasn't sure, but said he'd try. Since Greg was in the habit of reacting to anger with fighting, we also needed to talk about what set him off and how he could manage his anger. Although he had a few setbacks, Greg became more comfortable not fighting. He also found some new friends who didn't fight at the slightest provocation. His changed behavior meant that he was allowed to do weekly activities and finally he was cleared to start his driving lessons. Vowing to do whatever was necessary to get his driver's license, Greg virtually gave up fighting.

To get an idea about how well your teen's doing controlling his behavior, go over how often you're disciplining your teen now compared with one or two months ago. If your teen isn't losing points, isn't getting privileges taken away as much, and/or isn't being grounded as much, then he's improving and learning to control his behavior.

HAS YOUR TEEN'S OUTLOOK IMPROVED?

When her parents are encouraging and supportive, a teen is more likely to be calmer and happier. When she doesn't worry as much about making mistakes and getting criticized for trying things, she feels less anxious. When she feels capable, she's empowered.

When a teen feels as though her home is a place where promises are kept, it's a good feeling. By now your teen should know that when you say something, you're likely to mean it and to follow through, whether it's with a reward for good behavior or a discipline technique for problem behavior. Over time, this kind of follow-through helps to build trust and respect between you and your teen.

Making good on your word creates an atmosphere of predictability and stability. In a world where there's so much unpredictability, your teen needs to experience at least some certainty at home with parents upon whom she can count to do what they say, parents who will try to be fair and understanding. Using a positive-based contract can go a long way toward creating and maintaining this kind of atmosphere.

Of course, using a contract won't remove all the stress in your teen's life. That would be impossible and undesirable—it's not realistic for your teen to go through life with rose-colored glasses on. Still, it's nice if she can enjoy herself at least some of the time as she grows up.

In some situations, a contract is simply not enough and your teen will need additional help. The next chapter looks at circumstances that call for extra outside professional help.

13

Deciding If Your Teen Needs More Help

While a behavior contract can go a long way in addressing your concerns about your teen, there are situations in which you need to seek outside help. No matter how hard parents try, sometimes things get out of hand and they need to take action. For example, if your teen is involved in substance abuse, truancy, or delinquency, get some outside help. If your teen suffers from an eating disorder; displays frequent sadness, anger, or withdrawal; and/or talks about suicide, get help now! If you and your teen have such a stressful relationship that you can't be around one another and avoid each other whatever the cost, you need some help.

A first step is to talk with your family doctor, school counselor, or religious adviser. If none of these is available in the middle of the night, try the crisis hotline or the local hospital.

If you're scared, trust your intuition. In fact, err on the side of overreacting.

If you've taken stock and decided that your teen isn't making the progress you had hoped for, particularly in certain troubled areas, you should think about getting some extra help. Don't feel bad if your teen needs extra guidance; most teens need special assistance from time to time. Some problems can't be solved without special help.

In my clinical experience, since each teen and each situation is unique, there are no hard and fast rules about when you should or shouldn't pursue outside help. To help you make your decision, I've included some examples of what happened as my clients and I pondered getting extra help for their teenagers. As you'll see, sometimes we simply gave the problem more time to go away, and other times we fine-tuned the contract a bit. Still other times we reached out to other professionals in the community. Hopefully, the following scenarios will provide you with guidance as you consider getting extra help for your teen.

When Teens Need Outside Professional Help

Schoolwork Difficulties. If your teen can't concentrate long enough to finish her assignments or she tries but she still can't learn the material, you should consider getting extra help. Certain subject areas like reading or math may be especially difficult for her. If you suspect that your teen may have a learning problem, share your concerns with her teacher and school counselor and ask for their help. Although many learning problems are picked up before a child becomes an adolescent, this isn't always the case. So if your teen persists in having problems with schoolwork, don't talk yourself out of exploring the possibility that your teen has learning difficulties. Your teen's teacher may recommend testing to determine what is interfering with her ability to learn. Alternatively, you may decide your teen needs individual tutoring that focuses on the problems she is having. Let's see how Joyce Mallet used these ideas to get some additional help for her 12-year-old son, Steve.

> Although Joyce had been using a contract for a few weeks, using short study periods didn't seem to be helping Steve to sit down and read for more than 15 minutes. Joyce was getting more and more frustrated, especially because this approach was working well with her older daughter, Patty, 14. Joyce wondered what was wrong with Steve. To clarify what was going on, Joyce and I met with Steve's teacher and school counselor. Together we decided that it would be a good idea if the school psychologist gave Steve a few tests to double-check his reading level and to determine if he had any learning problems. After testing him, the school psychologist suggested that Steve be evaluated by a psychiatrist for attention deficit disorder. After a consultation, the psychiatrist recommended that Steve be given a trial of a stimulant medication used to treat attention deficit disorder. The medication was to help Steve concentrate. The psychiatrist also recommended weekly tutoring sessions and continued adherence to the structured contract Joyce had been using. This three-pronged approach helped Steve improve his reading and concentration. Remember that sometimes a disorder such as ADD isn't picked up until middle school when reading and academics become more difficult.

Obstinate, Stubborn, and Oppositional Behavior. Although most teens go through periods of being self-centered and impossible to get along with, if your teen always refuses to talk to and/or get along with you and the rest of the family, he may benefit from outside help. So if, in spite of your attempts to use the contract with your teen, she seems incapable of making any compromises and insists on getting her own way no matter what, consider getting some professional advice from your pediatrician or a mental health counselor on how to help her. Let's see what my clients the Ralstons did in this situation.

> Renee Ralston, 12, and her parents, Marty and Alex, were constantly fighting over something. It seemed to her parents that Renee always wanted her own way and was completely unwilling to compromise. Before her contract, Marty and Alex usually gave in to their daughter to avoid a blowup. Now, with the contract they were standing their ground, rewarding compliance, and setting limits. Although these techniques had helped considerably, the Ralstons still didn't feel as though they could really communicate with Renee. No matter how patient they tried to be, Renee would set them off—and their attempts to talk and listen would go up in smoke. Together we decided that the whole family should meet with me to work specifically on communication. In addition, I agreed to meet individually with Renee to give her a chance to tell me her side of the story and to help her learn how to compromise and be more flexible. The first few weeks were rocky, but gradually, by working together, everyone was able to get along better.

Depression and Suicidal Thoughts. Teenagers are famous for their moodiness. It goes with the territory. They're known to experience fluctuations between ecstasy and despair based on significant events such as whether their new boyfriend/girlfriend has called. These changes in mood are normal. However, if your teen is always unhappy, he may be depressed. Here are some other signals that your teen may suffer from depression: She feels worthless and hopeless, sleeps too much or hardly at all, does things slowly, and complains of having no energy. In addition, her appetite may have disappeared and her voice may sound flat and without affect.

In some depressions, your teen may become agitated and almost hyperactive, perhaps in part to distract herself from how bad she's feeling. She may think about and talk about committing suicide.

Although depression may sound like self-indulgence, it's a serious and very painful disorder. In some cases it is so painful that suicide, and thus the end to the pain, seems the only way out. I have never worked with a depressed teen who was using depression as a way to manipulate her parents. And each depressed teen felt to a certain degree that there was nothing that could be done. Fortunately, thanks to today's antidepressant medications, there's much that can be done.

If you suspect your teen may be depressed, visit your family doctor and/or get a referral to a psychiatrist who specializes in treating depression. If your teen has even hinted about suicide, call your physician, the local hospital, the community hotline, or suicide prevention line. Do it *now*. You have an emergency on your hands. It is not true that people who talk about suicide don't commit suicide. People who talk about suicide are often actively thinking about suicide but still hoping there's another answer. Help them find the answer by taking action. Teens with major depressive disorder usually respond well to the currently available antidepressant medications. Thus I always refer anyone with suspected depression to a psychiatrist for further evaluation.

> Although Becky, 15, loved her contract, her sister, Samantha, 17, didn't seem to care if she earned any rewards or activities. Samantha seemed down in the dumps. Her parents, Debbie and Ted, had done everything they could think of to cheer their daughter up. Debbie took her shopping and bought her a new

outfit and her current favorite compact disk. Ted spent extra time with her. But nothing helped. She didn't even seem happy when her friends came over. Debbie and I agreed that something must be wrong with Samantha. When Samantha came to talk to me, she told me she didn't know why but she was tired and sad all the time. Her mood worried me. As a first step I recommended Samantha visit her doctor for a checkup to determine if she had any physical problems that might be contributing to her mood. A physical exam and lab test revealed that Samantha was fine physically. After a consultation with a psychiatrist, Samantha was put on an antidepressant. Within a month her spirits had brightened considerably. Samantha continued to visit her psychiatrist on a monthly basis to monitor her progress.

If your teen seems depressed, take her seriously. Teens do not want to be depressed. Although you should expect your teen to be down in the dumps occasionally, if he is sad most of the time, even when good things are happening, don't hesitate, get some help.

Anxiety, Shyness, and Fearfulness. It can be very difficult for a parent to deal with a teen who is afraid to try anything new and often seems almost paralyzed by fear. If your teen seems scared of everything, talk to her doctor or counselor about how she can be helped. Keep in mind that frequently this kind of problem will improve if you are patient and introduce your teen to each new change very gradually.

Mary Jo shared with me that she had hoped her son Bruce would outgrow his fearfulness and timidity. But he was about to enter middle school and was still riddled with anxieties about all the changes he'd be going through. As a first step, we decided to help Bruce get familiar with his new school. He and his

mom visited the school and walked around. They
went into an empty classroom. They met the
principal. Next, Bruce took his younger sister Tammy
to the school and showed her around and explained
what he had learned. Mary Jo was thrilled with the
success of gradually exposing Bruce to new and
unfamiliar experiences. She planned to continue this
approach throughout the school year.

Eating Disorders. Eating disorders such as anorexia nervosa and
bulimia are conditions that definitely require professional help.
Anorexia refers to an illness in which your teen is starving
herself. If left untreated, it can be fatal. If your daughter is
perilously thin, exercises compulsively, and worries over every
bite she takes, she may very well be suffering from anorexia.
Young girls in particular are likely to be overly concerned with
body image, aspiring to be tall and thin, to look like the latest
model/actress of the week. However, when they lose touch with
their body image and perceive themselves as fat even when
they're wasting away, it's time to get help. If your daughter
binges and then purges or takes massive doses of laxatives to rid
her body of the calories she's just ingested, she's likely suffering
from bulimia and needs help as well. It can be difficult to
determine whether or not your teen is bulimic because she may
not be underweight. However, if you suspect that she might be
bulimic, a visit to the family doctor is crucial. Express your
concerns to your physician so that he can be attuned to the
telltale physical symptoms. If he feels there's a possibility of an
eating disorder, get a referral to a specialized eating-disorders
treatment program. You'll need clarification of what's going on.
In my experience, a contract that rewards eating will not work
in this case. Don't attempt to solve a complicated problem like
anorexia or bulimia on your own. Get help immediately.

No Friends. In spite of your efforts, if your teen just can't make
friends and is miserable because no one likes her, it's a good

idea to get input from other adults who spend time around her. Try to find out what she's doing that is turning the other teens off and what can be done to help her. You can watch her yourself. Social skills are such a nuanced set of behaviors; I recommend you consider short-term counseling to help your teen learn the details of getting along with other teens. In most cases you're too close to your teen's problem to be able to help her.

Out-of-Control and/or Antisocial/Addictive Behaviors. In spite of your efforts and your contract, if your teen is doing drugs and/or alcohol, failing school, hanging out with an unacceptable crowd, missing school, risking pregnancy or sexually transmitted disease, or talking about homicide or other forms of violence, you need to get some immediate outside help. If your teen chronically lies to you, steals things from you, or gets in serious fights, find some professional help before you end up visiting him in jail. If you need assistance, it doesn't mean you or your child failed at some crucial point in your relationship. It simply means you and your teen need assistance. Don't put your head in the sand and pretend it's going to get better all on its own, because there's a 99 percent chance it will get worse. There's help out there. I can tell you whom to call, but *you* have to make the call. Please do so for your teen and yourself.

Remember, it's up to you to seek help when your teen needs it. When you're worried about your teen, don't keep it to yourself. Share your concerns with a friend who can offer you a kind and understanding ear. And as a general rule of thumb, as a first step, it's always a good idea to consult with your teen's doctor when you have a concern. He or she is aware of your child's developmental history and can help you evaluate current problems and find help.

No matter whom you seek for help, keep in mind that pediatricians, teachers, school counselors, psychologists, social workers, and other professionals are there to provide services to you and your teen. So don't feel uncomfortable or think that you're inappropriately taking up someone's time. When you have a question, ask it and let them do their job by giving you an answer.

If you do decide to get extra help, be selective. It's important that you work with people with whom you feel comfortable. You need to trust them to do the right thing. Always let the person you're working with know that you've been using a contract. Explain the contract so they know how it works. Don't stop using your contract unless the professional who is helping you advises you to do so. Usually continuing your contract makes other types of help even more successful—whether the therapy is medication, counseling, testing, or tutoring.

If you feel your teen needs professional help for any of the problems mentioned above, please refer to Appendix C, which lists general guidelines and agencies you can contact as a starting point in your search for guidance and assistance.

No matter what you decide about getting extra help, don't shelve the idea of a contract, at least not permanently. A proactive, positive contract with explicit rules and limits can be helpful no matter how serious your teen's problems. The next chapter provides some guidelines to keep in mind as you use your contract over the years.

14

Looking Ahead

As you continue using your contract with your teen from month to month and year to year, it's a good idea to look back over this book periodically and review ideas about revising the rules, the rewards, the discipline, and the format of your contract. This review will help ensure that your contract is meeting the needs of your teen and your family. In addition, here are some general guidelines to follow as you keep your contract up and running.

KEEP SUPPORTING YOUR TEEN

Continue using encouragement, praise, and rewards. Although someday you may stop using a contract, you should never quit using the basics. For example, make rewarding good behaviors a habit you carry with you forever. Don't fall into the trap of taking good behavior for granted. If you stop letting your teen know what a good job she's doing, she may stop doing a good job.

Make sure everyone, yourself included, has a treat or a goal to anticipate. Whether or not you're still using a formal contract, your family needs to look forward to things. Plan pleasant, fun things for the family to do together.

STAY IN CONTACT WITH YOUR TEEN

Continue your talk times, and *don't* lose contact with your child. No matter how busy you are, spend at least some time each day talking with your teen. If no one feels like talking, do something you enjoy together. Most teens want to talk provided that this time is relaxed and no demands are made. Let's see how Rosa Perez found time to talk with her daughter in spite of both their busy schedules.

> Even though her family seemed to be on the go from morning to night, Rosa was determined to spend some time each day talking with and listening to her 14-year-old daughter, Dara. Some days the only time they had was in the car driving to and from school. Rosa made sure to use these times to connect with her daughter. In the morning she'd ask Dara what was up for the coming day. After they got comfortable with each other, they both enjoyed using humor. For example, Rosa might ask Dara what was on the threat board that day. Dara in return might answer in code; e.g., a battle was a quiz and a war was a test. As time went on they developed their own shorthand that allowed them to see the humor in most situations. Fortunately Dara felt comfortable talking to her mom—especially when things were bothering her—because she could count on her mom's support and help.

Treat Your Teen as the Unique Emerging Person She Is

Don't lose sight of your teen's own particular mix of talents and shortcomings. Don't fall into the trap of comparing your teen to other teenagers.

Each teen has her own developmental timetable. Your teen may develop quickly in one area but not in another. Or she may develop slowly in almost all areas. Each teen is different. Don't push or expect too much too soon. Give your teen the time, patience, and encouragement she needs to develop at her own speed. Growing up requires gradually mastering a series of skills. Make sure you're going slow and allowing her enough time.

Be Patient with Chronic Problems

When it comes to longstanding bad habits, try to be patient. In your contract you may want to try rewarding improvement in these chronic problems with something special. For example, if your teen has a long history of homework problems, you may need to offer a reward that results from her completing her schoolwork. Once it sinks in that the only way to stay up later is by doing her schoolwork, she'll most likely get to work.

Pick Your Battles Carefully

Don't attack every little thing that bothers you and try to fix it. As a general rule, stay away from interfering where personal taste is involved, e.g., hair, music, clothes, and room décor.

Don't Hesitate to Intervene

If your teen is in trouble, find some help to get him out of the ditch he's digging before it's too late.

Don't Give Up on Your Teen

You're his best hope. Without you he is a ship lost at sea. Do whatever you have to, but don't abandon him or throw in the towel. If you have an awful day or a horrible week, don't give up. Remember that every family has a truly terrible day from time to time. When this happens in your family, it's important to be as calm as you can and not overreact. Sometimes you won't be able to help yourself and before you know it you'll be screaming, yelling, pouting, withdrawing, or stomping around. When this happens, be sure to apologize to your family, explain why you blew up, wipe the slate clean, and keep the contract going. Don't dwell on awful days. Acknowledge them, try to learn from them, and then leave them in the past where they belong. Let's see how my client Roberto came unraveled over the small matter of his teens' skateboards.

> What a day it had been for Roberto. Nothing had gone right at his job and someone almost crashed into him on the drive home. So when he saw his teens' skateboards in the driveway again, he lost it. As they heard their dad screaming from the car, Juan and Anita knew they were in trouble. Running outside they got their gear out of the way in record speed. But that didn't seem to calm their dad down. He was still furious as he stormed into the house and barked, "How can you two be so irresponsible and thoughtless? Can't you even remember to put your stuff away? Isn't that simple enough? You're grounded. No television or friends for a month." At this point Juan and Anita retreated to their rooms. Their dad needed a chance to calm down. At dinner, Roberto explained to them that he'd had a bad day and that their skateboards were the final straw. But now that he'd had time to think about it, he realized

that he'd overreacted and that grounding didn't seem like the right thing to do. Together they agreed that if they left their skateboards in the driveway again they'd lose the chance to use them for the next day. Having patched things up, Roberto regrouped and, much to his surprise, had a pleasant evening with his teenagers. After Roberto shared this story with me, I congratulated him on being able to apologize to his teens and make amends for "losing it." I let him know that every parent overreacts from time to time and that the most important thing is to acknowledge this and set the record straight.

Don't Be Surprised If Not Everyone Loves the Idea of a Contract

There always seems to be at least one relative or friend who just can't accept the idea of a contract. Your teen's grandmother may insist that your contract is wrong because you're bribing your teen to do things he should want to do on his own. Your teen's uncle may insist that you're spoiling the kid with rewards and not being strict enough. Whatever they claim, stick to your plan. Remember, you know what is best for your teen and you're doing it. That's what counts.

Maintain Your Sense of Humor

Although parenting a teenager without a positive contract is difficult, I find that parenting without a sense of humor is impossible. Finding something funny is a great way to keep things in perspective. So try to lighten up and encourage the family to laugh a little.

YOUR CONTRACT IS ALWAYS THERE TO AID YOU

Even if you quit using your contract for a while, you can always start it up again and it will work. So as time goes by don't forget about it. Keep it in the back of your mind. If and when you need it again, get it started and watch it help.

CONTINUE YOUR CELEBRATIONS

I also recommend that parents and teens alike celebrate their efforts on a regular basis and acknowledge their hard work. Go out to eat together. Watch mindless entertainment on the television. Rent a movie. Spend some nonstressed time together, laughing and commiserating face to face. Before you know it, your teen will be out of the house and driving you crazy on the telephone or by E-mail about her college or job exploits . . . but that's an entirely different book, now, isn't it?

Take advantage of the fact that your teen is still home and that you can still share some time together. Remember, even the best parents in the world need all the luck they can get to keep their teen from driving them crazy. Good luck!

APPENDIX A

Forms to Copy

Feel free to copy these forms for your use.

Contract Rule Checklist

Contract Reward Checklist

Contract Reward System

Parent Reward Checklist

Contract Discipline Worksheet

Comprehensive Contract: Safety and School Rules

Comprehensive Contract: Family Rules

Brief General Contract

Limited Contract

Contract Rule Checklist

Instructions: Check the rules you want to include in your teen's contract. You can use the space next to each rule to define the rule more specifically.

Safety Rules

- ☐ Give advance notice of plans.
- ☐ Check in.
- ☐ Keep curfew.
- ☐ Engage in agreed-upon activities:

  _____
  _____
  _____
  _____

- ☐ Other rules:

  _____
  _____

School Rules

- ☐ Be on time.
- ☐ Attend all classes.
- ☐ Behave appropriately.
- ☐ Complete assignments on time.
- ☐ Get passing grades.
- ☐ Other rules:

  _____
  _____

Family Rules

- ☐ Get up and ready in the morning.
- ☐ Maintain room.
- ☐ Do other chores.
- ☐ Get along with family members (parents and siblings).
- ☐ Follow through.
- ☐ Behave nicely at mealtimes.
- ☐ Comply with bedtime schedule.
- ☐ Other rules:

  _____
  _____

Contract Reward Checklist

Instructions: Check each reward you are willing to include in your teen's contract. Keep in mind that you'll be discussing the specifics of these rewards when you're in contract negotiations with your teen. The blank spaces are included for any additional rewards you or your teen think of during negotiations.

Weekday Rewards

Activities
- ☐ 15 minutes of free time.
- ☐ Talk on the phone.
- ☐ Play computer game.
- ☐ Listen to music.
- ☐ Watch television.
- ☐ _____
- ☐ _____
- ☐ _____
- ☐ _____

After school and/or evening activities
- ☐ _____
- ☐ _____
- ☐ _____

Bedtime
- ☐ Stay up 30 minutes later.
- ☐ _____

Points
- ☐ Turned in for money.
- ☐ As credit toward future activity/purchase.
- ☐ _____

Weekend Rewards

Activities afternoon/evening
- ☐ Go to a friend's house.
- ☐ Have friend(s) over.
- ☐ Go to the mall.
- ☐ See a movie.
- ☐ Shop.
- ☐ Attend a party.
- ☐ Be driven someplace.
- ☐ Drive.
- ☐ Other entertainment events.
- ☐ _____
- ☐ _____
- ☐ Make a purchase.
- ☐ _____
- ☐ _____

Monthly Rewards
- ☐ _____
- ☐ _____

Contract Reward System

Instructions: Beside each of the contract rules listed below, indicate the type or number of rewards that can be earned.

Following school and safety rules
    = ___ weekday activities
    = ___ weekend activities

These activities will be chosen by you and your teen on a weekly basis.

Schoolwork bonuses

Doing homework for ___ minutes = ___ minutes of free time or ___ points.

Finishing homework = staying up ___ minutes later or ___ points.

Avoiding last-minute frenzy = ___ points.

Following family rules

Getting ready in the morning = ___ point(s).

Maintaining room by ___ P.M. = ___ point(s).

Doing other chores = ___ point(s) per chore.

Getting along with parents in the morning, in the afternoon, at dinnertime, and in the evening = ___ point(s) for each time period.

Getting along with siblings in the morning, in the afternoon, at dinnertime, and in the evening = ___ point(s) for each time period.

Following through = ___ point(s) each time.

Behaving nicely at mealtime = ___ point(s).

Complying with bedtime schedule = ___ point(s).

Other rules
    _____ = _____ point(s).
    _____ = _____ point(s).

Each point = ___ cents.
        = _____ credit(s) toward an activity.
        = _____ credit(s) toward a purchase.

You and your teen will decide together on the activities and purchases that points can earn. The point or credit value of each activity or purchase will be discussed/negotiated by you and your teen.

Parent Reward Checklist

Instructions: The following list includes rewards that parents enjoy. Check off/circle those activities and things you'd like to have as rewards. Add any others you might think of.

Daily Rewards

- ☐ Take a walk, get some exercise.
- ☐ Watch television, write a letter, talk to a friend, listen to music.
- ☐ Read a book, look at the newspaper, flip through a magazine.
- ☐ Use the computer, learn about something new.
- ☐ Cook, sew, garden.
- ☐ Work on car, home-improvement project.
- ☐ Just do nothing for a few moments.
- ☐ Other.

Weekly Rewards

- ☐ Try to get away for a few hours, go somewhere, do something.
- ☐ Go out for dinner, see a movie, go shopping.
- ☐ Play a sport, go on a long walk.
- ☐ Do something fun or just do nothing at all.
- ☐ Other.

Contract Discipline Worksheet

Instructions: Check each rule listed below that you are concerned your teen may not be able to follow. Make a note of the discipline techniques you plan to use. Remember, whenever possible, use the techniques of ignoring, warnings, and/or withholding a reward before invoking more heavy-duty consequences such as prohibiting an activity, restricting curfew, or grounding your teen.

Not following safety rules

- ☐ Not giving advance notice of plans
- ☐ Not checking in
- ☐ Not keeping curfew
- ☐ Not engaging in agreed-upon activities
- ☐ Not following other rules

Not following school rules

- ☐ Not being on time
- ☐ Not attending all classes
- ☐ Not behaving appropriately
- ☐ Not completing assignments on time
- ☐ Not getting passing grades
- ☐ Not following other rules

Not following family rules

- ☐ Not getting ready in the morning
- ☐ Not maintaining room
- ☐ Not doing chores
- ☐ Not getting along with parents
- ☐ Not getting along with siblings
- ☐ Not following through
- ☐ Not behaving nicely at mealtimes
- ☐ Not complying with bedtime schedule
- ☐ Not following other rules

Comprehensive Contract
Safety and School Rules

Safety Rules

	M	T	W	Th	F	Sa	Sun
☐ Give advance notice of plans.							
☐ Check in.							
☐ Keep curfew.							
☐ Engage in agreed-upon activities:							
_____							
_____							
_____							
_____							
☐ Other rules:							
_____							
_____							

School Rules

	M	T	W	Th	F	Sa	Sun
☐ Be on time.							
☐ Attend all classes.							
☐ Behave appropriately.							
☐ Complete assignments on time.							
☐ Get passing grades.							
☐ Other rules:							
_____							
_____							

Complying with all safety and school rules each day earns the privilege of getting to participate in _____ after-school activities and _____ weekend activities. Activities to choose from this week are:

    Weekday activities: _____

    Weekend activities: _____

Bonuses for complying with the school rules:

Doing schoolwork or spending time reading or learning for _____ minutes = _____ minutes of free time or _____ points.

Finishing schoolwork earns staying up _____ minutes later or _____ points. Preparing ahead of time and completing work without last-minute hassles = _____ points.

I, _____ , agree to follow the rules listed above in return for which I will be compensated as noted.

Signed _____ Date _____

I/We, _____ , the parent(s) of _____ , agree to honor the terms of this contract and provide compensation as noted.

Signed _____ Date _____

Comprehensive Contract
Family Rules

Family Rules

	M	T	W	Th	F	Sa	Sun

☐ Getting ready = ___ pt(s).
☐ Maintaining room = ___ pt(s).
☐ Other chores:

    _____ = ___ pt(s).
    _____ = ___ pt(s).
    _____ = ___ pt(s).

☐ Getting along with parents
    morning = ___ pt(s).
    afternoon = ___ pt(s).
    dinnertime = ___ pt(s).
    evening = ___ pt(s).

☐ Getting along with siblings
    morning = ___ pt(s).
    afternoon = ___ pt(s).
    dinnertime = ___ pt(s).
    evening = ___ pt(s).

☐ Following through
    = ___ pt(s) each time.

☐ Behaving nicely at mealtimes
    = ___ pt(s).

☐ Complying with bedtime
    schedule = ___ pt(s).

☐ Other rules:

    _____
    _____

Total points earned per day: _____

Total points earned per week: _____

Value of points: 1 point = ___ cents/ ___ credits toward activity/purchase.

Ideas about how to spend points:

    Free time: ___ minutes free time costs ___ points.

    Future activity and cost in credits:

        _____ costs ___ credits.
        _____ costs ___ credits.

    Future purchase and cost in credits:

        _____ costs ___ credits.
        _____ costs ___ credits.

I, _____ , agree to follow the family rules listed above for which I will earn points and be compensated as noted.

Signed _____ Date _____

I/We, _____ , the parent(s) of _____ , agree to honor this contract and comply with its terms.

Signed _____ Date _____

Brief General Contract

I, _____ , agree to follow
    safety rules
    school rules
    and family rules

in return for which I will be allowed
    to continue enjoying approved activities
    and to be in charge of my own schedule.

Signed _____ Date _____

I/We, _____ , parent(s) of _____ ,
agree to abide by the terms of this contract.

Signed _____ Date _____

Limited Contract

I, _____ , agree to do the following: _____ for which I will be rewarded as follows: _____.

Signed _____ Date _____

I/We, _____ , the parent(s) of _____ , agree to offer the above reward as long as _____ does the following:

_____

Signed _____ Date _____

Appendix B

Further Reading

More About Teen Development

The following book is my pick for the best resource on overall physical, psychological, and social teenage development. It is easy to read and understand and full of good ideas and useful information.

Steinberg, Lawrence, and Ann Levine. *You and Your Adolescent: A Parent's Guide for Ages 10–20.* New York: Harper Perennial, 1997.

Two other good resources that take a look at the stages and development of adolescents are:

Elkind, David. *All Grown Up and No Place to Go: Teenagers in Crisis.* Reading, Massachusetts: Addison-Wesley, 1998.

Riera, Michael. *Uncommon Sense for Parents with Teenagers.* Berkeley, California: Celestial Arts, 1995.

More About Using Discipline with Teenagers

These books offer advice on how to cope with common but irritating teenage problems using practical methods. Each tends to focus on how to discipline teens after problems happen. They pay less attention to techniques to use to prevent or reduce problems before they get started in the first place.

Fleming, Don. *How to Stop the Battle with Your Teenager: A Practical Guide to Solving Everyday Problems.* New York: A Fireside Book, 1993.

Horn, Wade, and Carol Keough. *Better Homes and Gardens New Teen Book: An A–Z Guide for Parents of 9–16 Year Olds.* Des Moines, Iowa: Meredith Books, 1999.

Kelly, Kate. *The Complete Idiot's Guide to Parenting a Teenager.* New York: Alpha Books, 1996.

Phelan, Thomas. *Surviving Your Adolescents: How to Manage and Let Go of Your 13–18 Year Olds.* Glen Ellyn, Illinois: Child Management Inc., 1994.

More About Teaching Personal Responsibility

Eastman, M. *Taming the Dragon in Your Child: Solutions for Breaking the Cycle of Family Anger.* New York: John Wiley & Sons, Inc., 1994. This book looks at the sources of rage and how to anticipate and defuse your teen's anger.

Langford, Laurie. *The Big Talk: Talking to Your Child About Sex and Dating*. New York: John Wiley & Sons, Inc., 1998. This book shows parents how to have warm, nurturing conversations with their children about puberty, dating, relationships, and sex.

Lickona, Thomas. *Raising Good Children: From Birth Through the Teenage Years*. New York: Bantam Books, 1994. This book explores how to help your teen develop a lifelong sense of honesty, decency, and respect for others.

Windell, James. *Six Steps to an Emotionally Intelligent Teenager*. New York: John Wiley & Sons, Inc., 1999. This book focuses on teaching teens social skills including getting along with others, monitoring their own behavior, handling their anger, and solving conflicts on their own.

MORE ABOUT TREATING SPECIFIC, SERIOUS PROBLEMS AND DISORDERS

These books are somewhat more clinical in orientation, as they detail treatment for serious psychological disorders.

Kastner, Laura, and Jennifer Wyatt. *The Seven-Year Stretch: How Families Work Together to Grow Through Adolescence*. Boston: Houghton Mifflin Company, 1997. This book looks at the factors that influence the development of functional versus dysfunctional adolescents.

Pipher, Mary. *Reviving Ophelia: Saving the Selves of Adolescent Girls*. New York: Ballantine Books, 1994. This book looks at anorexia and bulimia in detail.

Sells, Scott. *Treating the Tough Adolescent: A Family-Based, Step-by-Step Guide*. New York: The Guilford Press, 1998.

This book is a must for any parent who has an out-of-control teen or any therapist who works with antisocial and/or substance-abusing teenagers.

MORE ABOUT USING A SIMILAR APPROACH WITH YOUNGER CHILDREN

If you have younger children and would like to use an approach similar to the proactive, positive behavior contract you're using with your teen, I recommend you get a copy of my first book, *How to Keep Your Kids from Driving You Crazy*, published by John Wiley & Sons, Inc., in 1997. This convenient guidebook will take you step-by-step through the process of creating a Behavior Game for children ages 2 through 12. You'll learn how to motivate your kids to behave better, get along with others, and misbehave less often. Like the contracts you learned about in this book, the Behavior Game is based on scientific research and over 25 years of my own experience as a clinical psychologist and mother of two boys. Thousands of families have found the Behavior Game to be a fun and effective way to improve their children's behavior.

Appendix C

Getting Professional Help

Finding a professional who can help your teen is likely to take some time and effort. In my work as a psychologist, I've found that no matter how elaborate and thorough a referral system I develop, I need to revise and add to it constantly—partly because my clients have ever-changing needs and partly because the existing resources change so quickly. As a general rule, don't hurry your help-seeking process. Spend time weighing your options and deciding on the best way to get started. However, if you're faced with an emergency, an acute situation in which there's danger for your teen or others—such as suicidal behavior—take immediate action. Call your doctor or your local hospital.

As you learned in Chapter 13, the best place to begin your search for help is usually with professionals who currently care for your teen. Ask your teen's doctor for advice and referrals. If she's stumped, try contacting your teen's teacher or school counselor. Many parents find it helpful to talk with friends, especially those who have consulted a specialist for similar problems. If you're involved in a community activity, church, temple, or synagogue, check with the staff to find out if they have a recommendation about who can help you.

The phone book can prove helpful. Currently many phone books contain a section on local health and mental health services as well as hotlines to call in emergencies. These up-to-date listings of community services can give you a place to call and get started in your search. If you have a local mental health association, you can contact it for referrals as well. If none of these avenues works, consider contacting national or state associations for their ideas and recommendations. These organizations list members by location and specialization. Here is a list of associations you may find helpful:

American Academy of Pediatrics
141 Northwest Point Blvd.
Elk Grove Village, IL 60007
(708) 228-5005

American Psychological Association
750 First Street, NE
Washington, DC 20002
(800) 374-2721

National Association of Social Workers
750 First Street, NE, Suite 700
Washington DC 20002
(800) 638-8799

American Psychiatric Association
1400 K Street, NW
Washington DC 20005
(202) 682-6000

Association for Children/Teenagers with
  Learning Disabilities
4156 Library Road
Pittsburgh, PA 15234
(412) 341-1515

Attention Deficit Information Network, Inc.
472 Hillside Avenue
Needham, MA 02194
(617) 455-9895

American Anorexic/Bulimia Association
293 Central Park West, #1R
New York, NY 10024
(201) 501-8351

Don't put your head in the sand and hope your teen's problems will magically go away. If your teen needs help, get it.

Be patient, creative, persistent, and optimistic as you search. Help is just around the corner. Good luck in your search. I've got my fingers crossed and know you'll keep looking because, after all, your teen is worth it.

Appendix D

Foundations of the Contract

The following books and articles helped shape the proactive, positive contract you've learned how to use in this text. These references contain research studies, clinical case studies, and/or current statistical facts, all of which influenced the step-by-step approach advocated in this book.

Bandura, A. *Social Foundations of Thought and Action: A Social Cognitive Theory.* Englewood Cliffs, New Jersey: Prentice Hall, 1986.

Bandura, A. *Social Learning Theory.* Englewood Cliffs, New Jersey: Prentice Hall, 1977.

Kantrowitz, Barbara, and Pat Wingert. "The Secret Lives of Teens," *Newsweek,* May 10, 1999.

Maccoby, Eleanor, and John Martin. "Socialization in the Context of the Family: Parent–Child Interaction," in

P. H. Mussen, ed., *The Handbook of Child Psychology,* 4th ed. New York: Wiley, 1983.

Masten, Ann, and J. Douglas Coatsworth. "The Development of Competence in Favorable and Unfavorable Environments: Lessons from Research on Successful Children," *American Psychologist,* February 1998.

Meichenbaum, D. *Cognitive-Behavior Modification.* New York: Plenum Publishing, 1977.

Mischel, W. *Introduction to Personality.* New York: Holt, Rinehart and Winston, 1971.

Mischel, W. *Personality and Assessment.* New York: John Wiley & Sons, 1968.

Mischel, W. "Toward a Cognitive Social Learning Reconceptualization of Personality," *Psychological Review* 80: 252–283, 1973.

O'Leary, K. D., and G. T. Wilson. *Behavior Therapy: Outcome and Application* (2d ed.). Englewood Cliffs, New Jersey: Prentice Hall, 1987.

Rosenthal, T. L. "Social Learning Theory and Behavior Therapy," in G. T. Wilson and C. M. Franks, eds., *Contemporary Behavior Therapy: Conceptual and Empirical Foundations.* New York: Guilford Press, 1987.

Ullmann, L. P., and L. Krasner, eds., *Case Studies in Behavior Modification.* New York: Holt, Rinehart and Winston, 1965.

Index